Soaps

Soaps

ELAINE STAVERT

GUILD OF MASTER
CRAFTSMAN PUBLICATIONS

First published 2009 by
Guild of Master Craftsman Publications Ltd
Castle Place, 166 High Street,
Lewes, East Sussex BN7 1XU

Reprinted 2010, 2012

ISBN: 978-1-86108-645-7

Associate Publisher: Jonathan Bailey
Production Manager: Jim Bulley
Managing Editor: Gerrie Purcell
Project Editor: Virginia Brehaut
Editors: Alison Howard and Gill Parris
Managing Art Editor: Gilda Pacitti
Designer: Jo Patterson
Picture Researcher: Hedda Roennevig

Set in Gill Sans and Ribbon

Colour origination by **GMC Reprographics**
Printed and bound in China by C&C Offset

Why we love soaps

Splashing with water, creating a lather
A natural soap: I know I would rather!
By making my own for family and friends,
A luxurious time I know they will spend.

With recipes fashioned to soften and soothe,
And exotic aromas, inspiring the mood
For an evening relaxing, an ideal aim
After working all day or a tennis game.

Present all your loved ones with gorgeous soap
And encourage the children to bathe (you hope!)
So that hours in the bath may now be spent
With sumptuous bars in your favourite scent.

Use an artistic palette of imagination
To mould and to shape a unique creation
In the shades of a rainbow or kaleidoscope
You too will find out why we love making soap.

*C*ontents

5

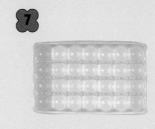
6

7

8

9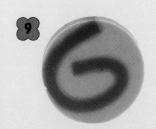

10

11

12

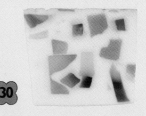

Introduction

Have you ever really looked at a bar of soap and wondered exactly what it is, how it is made and why it cleans us? Most of us take care with the food we eat, but tend not to be aware of what we are putting on our largest organ, the skin. We take many of the toiletries that we use today for granted and tend not to read the ingredients on their packaging, or, if we do, we are mystified by the strange Latin names and chemicals listed.

To use a scented herbal soap is to partake of an element of ritual used down the centuries. Since time immemorial aromatic oils, perfumes and herbs have been used to cleanse, anoint and scent the body for hygiene, medicinal purposes, worship and spiritual wellbeing. The latest ready-to-use 'melt and pour' soap bases are fast and easy to use, making it easy to craft, mould and shape fantastic vegetable glycerine soaps. The results need be limited only by your imagination.

What exactly is soap?

Soap is a surfactant, or 'surface-active agent', which works by reducing surface tension between two substances. It is usually made in solid bars and is used with water for washing and cleaning. Soap is made by combining oil or fat (fatty acid) – any type of vegetable oil including coconut, palm, olive and sunflower – or animal fat (tallow) with an alkali – either sodium hydroxide/soda ash ($NaOH$) or potassium hydroxide/potash (KOH). The fat reacts with the alkali in a process called saponification, during which the fat molecules are transformed into alkali salts of the fatty acids. For instance, tallow becomes *sodium* tallowate and palm oil becomes *sodium* palmate. Many commercial soap products are made with animal fat.

Oil / fat (fatty acid) + alkali (sodium or potassium hydroxide) = soap

How does soap clean?

Simple dirt can just be washed off with water, but most dirty things are greasy and oily, too. All living and non-living things are made up of small particles called molecules. Oil and water molecules will not stick to each other, but both will stick to soap molecules. A soapy lather will therefore attract both water and oil, and hold on to the molecules so they cannot separate until they are rinsed away – along with the dirt. Millions of micro-organisms live on the skin, including mites, yeasts and bacteria that may spread germs and diseases. Many of these are transferred by the hands, which we tend not to wash often enough or thoroughly enough. Soap and water can remove many of these nasties.

History of bathing

Bathing in water promotes feelings of comfort, security, peace and contentment.

No life form can survive without water (H$_2$O). Our bodies are around 75 per cent water, and water features at the moment of creation in the beliefs of many cultures. Bathing in water promotes feelings of comfort, security, peace and contentment, perhaps because it subconsciously reminds us of the protective time in our mother's womb.

Over the centuries, bathing has meant different things to different cultures. Some have completely scoured and cleansed their bodies, while others have declined even to dip a big toe into water. In ancient times most cultures believed that water was one of the divine forces of nature that, as a source of spiritual energy, would heal, cleanse and purify the spirit. Bathing in water was therefore used for religious ceremonies and to mark rites of passage rather than for cleaning the body.

It is difficult to tell which of the ancient civilisations was the first to bathe, but dirt and cleanliness have come in and out of fashion at different periods in history throughout the world. Bathing probably first took place in rivers, springs, pools, wells and reservoirs. Vapour bathing was another kind of cleansing ritual used in Russia, by early American Indians and by the Irish. It involved placing fire-heated stones inside a steam-tent or room and dousing them with water to create steam. This method has long been used by the Finns to create saunas. Japanese bathing rituals were – and still are – a cleansing of the body and the soul, a place for reflection, and a time for family in communal baths known as sentos, or onsen, that are often built round hot springs.

This method has long been used by the Finns to create saunas

Ancient Egyptians

Records show that the Egyptians were prolific bathers who spent hours on their ablutions. They bathed at home in a separate room, possibly using perfumed creams made from lime and oil. Afterwards they smothered themselves with aromatic oils to nourish and protect their skin.

Ancient Greeks

The Ancient Greeks used individual baths grouped around a main pool. Bathing was a social occasion and men would chat, play dice and perhaps have a drink and a snack. There were also rooms for cold and warm baths, which were similar but less sophisticated than the later Roman Baths. Baths were also available in the gymnasia used by wealthy upper-class Greeks. Here men oiled and dusted their naked bodies before exercising, playing ball games, or wrestling. Afterwards, they scraped down their sweaty, oily skin with a metal instrument and washed off the excess using unheated water from a bath or basin.

Roman baths

For Romans, splashing, soaking, steaming and oiling their bodies was part of everyday life. Life in those times was short; medicinal bathing was considered to be of great importance and a preventative for a vast range of illnesses. Most wealthy Romans had their own private baths, but for socializing they also used the public baths and spas, where Romans from all classes and walks of life spent much of their leisure time.

Turkish baths

Beautifully constructed marble Turkish baths called hamam were traditionally sited at mineral springs. These comprised three rooms: one with a steaming hot bath; a warm room for washing, and a cool room for resting and relaxation. The baths were social events for both rich and poor people. They were used by women to celebrate rites of passage such as weddings and births, religious holidays and to beautify themselves with the treatments on offer.

A Japanese communal bath.

The Muslims brought their bathing rituals and the concept of the bath to Turkey, mixed with the designs of the Roman bath.

During this period people believed that the linen of their clothes and bedding would absorb their dirt and perspiration, thereby keeping them clean. They used perfume and cologne to mask their scent.

But dirt was a sign of the average worker's station in life. Blacksmiths, tanners, chimney sweeps, farm workers and most ordinary people lived most of their lives with black fingernails and covered in dirt. As none of their contemporaries washed, their body odour went undetected; as everyone was smelly, nobody noticed.

From the late Georgian period people began to bathe for pleasure. In the early decades of the nineteenth century the use of the bath and bathing increased, thanks to the introduction of plumbing and running hot water. An increasing number of medical journals also advocated bathing for health benefits. From the 1820s, specialist bath manufacturers began to appear, and the patent for the

British bathing habits

A long period during which most people did not wash lasted from the late Middle Ages until the end of the seventeenth century, though a few hot public baths still existed. There were few facilities and little opportunity to immerse the body in water, except perhaps in rivers. Soap was rough and caustic and mainly used for laundry, and later on with the importation of olive oil from Europe, was an expensive and highly taxed luxury.

Roman Baths in Bath, England.

first shower bath was taken out in 1830. Recreational bathing increased with the coming of the railways and cheap excursion fares that made trips to the seaside more accessible.

By the early eighteenth century attitudes towards bathing had begun to change, and wealthy people washed in basins in their chambers using warm water brought by servants. They also began to travel to 'take the waters' at mineral spas including Tunbridge Wells, Epsom, Malvern and Bath, where they could also pamper themselves with manicures and other beauty treatments.

A version of the Turkish bath introduced to Victorian Britain was a contemporary version of a Roman hot air bath, and reminiscent of a sauna. The idea caught on and hundreds of Turkish baths opened all over Britain and in other parts of the Empire. By the beginning of the twentieth century people had discovered that cleanliness could help to beat the spread of disease, and many homes had bathrooms. But, increasingly, the pleasurable experience of immersing the body in a tub of warm, scented water has been replaced by a quick shower, the bathing equivalent of the fast food outlet.

An area of a Turkish bath (hamam) in Istanbul. A version of these baths was introduced to Britain in Victorian times.

So, next time you jump into your shower, stop to think what a warm, sensual, therapeutic soak in the tub with aromatic oils could do for your mind, body and spirit. Close your eyes, and let your mind drift back in time, remembering how our ancestors may have bathed in similar ways.

Victorian bathing machines

History of soap

Many legends refer to the invention of soap, and the word probably derives from the Latin 'sapo'. Even in prehistoric times, early man might have noticed that a strange soapy substance would form after a rainstorm around the remains of the fire on which meat had been cooked. This phenomenon would have been caused when the fats (fatty acids) from the meat mixed with the alkaline ashes of the fire. Early man did not, however, shower and shave around the campfire!

The earliest form of soap was probably made at home and used for cleaning wool to make textiles. It is likely to have been a paste-type substance made from animal fat or vegetable oil boiled with wood ash. A formula for soap made from water, alkali and cassia oil has been found on a Babylonian clay tablet dating from about 2200 BC.

A few hundred years ago soap was very smelly stuff. It was made by women on farms from leftover pieces of fat from cooking which had been stored up for many months. The animal fat was melted down in a big pot over a fire until it was liquid. Ash saved from the family fire over long periods of time was added to water to create an alkaline solution called lye. The lye was poured into the melted fat which caused the mixture to heat up; the mixture was stirred for several hours until thick and poured into wooden crates to harden. This quite nasty, harsh soap was mainly used for laundry, washing dishes and baths.

Soap making increased dramatically around the eighth century. Italy, Spain and France became centres of soap manufacturing because of their supply of raw materials such as olive oil. Soap-makers formed Guilds, which guarded their trade secrets closely. In many countries, soap was regarded as a luxurious item and taxed heavily. When this tax was removed, well into the nineteenth century, soap became available to ordinary people, and standards of cleanliness improved.

In 1791 French chemist Nicholas Leblanc patented a process that used salt to make sodium carbonate, an ingredient that is combined with fat and oils to produce soap. This enabled soap to be manufactured on a larger and cheaper scale. Twenty years later the science of modern soap making was born when another French chemist, Michel Eugene Chevreul, discovered the chemical nature of fats, glycerine and fatty acids. These discoveries, together with the development of power to operate factories, were a major step toward large-scale commercial soap making.

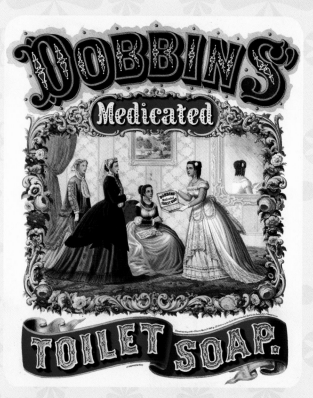

An 1869 advertisement for medicated soap.

How soap is made

Cold processed soap

Most small-scale handmade natural soaps are made by the 'cold processed' method. The oil or fat is gently heated until it is liquid, and an alkaline 'lye' solution of water plus sodium or potassium hydroxide is added. Once poured into the moulds the soap is insulated and the chemical reaction causes the soap to further heat up and, 24 hours later, it will be cool and set.

The bars are then cut and cured for up to six weeks to allow the saponification process to complete. During this time, the acid and alkali balance to a safe pH level, the water in the soap evaporates, and the bars harden. Glycerine is formed naturally from the oils and is retained in the soap, together with any excess fat incorporated in the recipe. This method uses up all the 'lye' or alkali to produce a superior bar that is mild, highly moisturizing and suitable for people with sensitive skin.

Hot processed soap

This historical method is similar to the cold processed method but once it starts to thicken the soap is cooked further, instead of being poured first and left to heat up. This accelerates saponification. The thick soap is then spooned into moulds and is ready to be used as soon as it has set, without curing.

Melt and pour soap

This uses a ready-cured vegetable glycerine base that is heated in a pan on top of a stove or in a microwave. Essential oils, fragrance, colour and herbs may be added to the melted hot soap, which can be skilfully handcrafted with multi-layering, swirls and embedded patterns.

Industrial soap making

Soap began to be more in demand at the end of the eighteenth and beginning of the nineteenth centuries, thanks to the abolition of the high 'luxury' tax on soap, and the medical profession's view that health could be improved and the spread of disease reduced by bathing and keeping clean. Large-scale factories began to appear; the A & F Pears Ltd factory opened in London in 1789, and theirs is claimed to be the earliest registered brand of soap. The company was famous for its distinctive advertising campaigns. During the First World War, meat was very difficult to obtain so there was not enough animal fat for soap making. This prompted the German invention of detergent, which derives from Latin and means 'wipe off'. Chemical detergent molecules grab oil and lather up quickly and easily, even in cold water. They are used for laundry and household cleaning, and are also added to soap bars and other toiletries, but are more powerful than real soap and can be very harsh and irritating to the skin. One of the most common ingredients used in these products is Sodium Lauryl Sulphate or Sodium Laureth Sulphate, a harsh chemical foamer. Many soap bars, liquid soaps and shower gels commercially produced today are technically detergents, rather than real soap, as they are made using fast and inexpensive methods. The precious glycerine is usually removed and used in creams and lotions instead.

Milled soaps (or French milled soaps)

Crude soap with added salt is boiled with water and milled through rollers. The glycerine is removed so the soap does not stick to the rollers, and the water from the soap is removed by drying. The resulting dry soap is made into pellets or noodles which are combined with fragrance and colour. The soap is then highly processed by pushing it through different screens, rollers, refiners, mills and chambers to produce a smooth hard bar.

Basic techniques

Equipment, soap base and moulds

To make the recipes in this book you will not need any complicated equipment. In fact you will probably already have most of the equipment that you need in your kitchen. You will, however, need to purchase the raw ingredients to make your soaps.

These are easily obtained from the growing number of mail order soap supplies companies. They will usually sell most, or even all, of the ingredients and moulds that you will need to make soaps for craft and hobby use (see the list of suggested suppliers on pages 148–151).

To make the recipes in this book you will need:

- 'Melt and pour' vegetable glycerine soap base
- Plastic bowl, saucepan or double boiler for melting the soap
- Plastic or glass measuring jug or weighing scales
- Set of teaspoon and tablespoon measures
- Plastic or metal spoons or spatulas to stir the melted soap base
- Kitchen knife for cutting loaves of soap
- Cutting board
- Moulds

- Small spray or spritz bottle filled with surgical spirit or rubbing alcohol
- Colour (optional)
- Fragrance or essential oils (optional)
- Herbs, glitters, oils and additives (optional)
- Ladle (optional)
- Plastic tray or box lid lined with a plastic bag
  Note: this is only necessary when using cookie cutters or making swirls
- Plastic food wrap or container to store the finished soaps

Soap bases

All the recipes in this book use a pre-made vegetable glycerine soap base which is gently heated until it is liquid. This soap base is generally known as 'melt and pour' or 'melt and mould' soap. Liquid colour, herbs, oils, glitter and scent may be added to the melted soap base, which is then simply poured or cast into a mould. It is left to set until hard and is then ready to use. Melt and pour soap bases can also be artistically handcrafted by layering, swirling and embedding various objects. Setting times will depend on the thickness of the bar, the quantity of additives, the type of soap base and the temperature of the base and the environment.

There are several types of soap bases made by various large suppliers. Below are details of some of the different bases you may find, and all good suppliers should be able to provide a full list of ingredients. Most of the following soap bases will have been made with coconut and palm oil, or derivatives of these vegetable oils, with added ingredients such as glycerine. Suppliers may also stock other bases including aloe vera, honey, shea butter and hemp. In humid or cold damp conditions, vegetable glycerine soaps may 'sweat' or attract moisture and 'low sweat' soap bases with reduced glycerine are sometimes available.

Basic/regular soap base	This is usually crystal clear and is ideal if you want to see embedded items, such as miniature soaps, pictures or other objects through the soap. It usually contains SLS (sodium lauryl sulphate), which may cause some skin irritation, but produces a frothy lather and has a good fragrance lift. It is also available in opaque white, which has added titanium dioxide.
Natural or SLS / SLES-free base	This has no added SLS (sodium lauryl sulphate) or SLES (sodium laureth sulphate) so should not cause skin irritation or affect sensitive skin. It is also usually free from surfactants or MPG (mono propylene glycol). It is a softer base with a slightly cloudier appearance than the regular clear soap base. It is very moisturizing and leaves the skin smooth and silky, but does not produce the same big lather as regular soap base.
Organic base	This is made from certified organic ingredients and is usually slightly yellow in colour. It is free from SLS and SLES, and does not produce the same big lather as regular soap base.
Olive oil base	This is translucent with a green tinge from the added olive oil and is softer than the regular base.
Goat's milk base	This has added goat's milk to moisturize.
Suspending base	This is useful if you want to suspend glitters, pumice, loofah, seeds, oats etc in your soap base.

Finding moulds

Many household objects or packaging from everyday life may be used as soap moulds. Any plastic mould may be used for making soap, as long as it has flexible sides to make removal easier.

Food packaging offers a wealth of suitable moulds, and next time you go shopping it will be hard to resist buying strange cheeses, unusual yoghurts and boxes of cookies just for their soap-moulding potential.

A selection of moulds found around the home.

Some of the household items that may be used for moulds:

- Empty margarine tub
- Plastic food container
- Flexible ice cube mould
- Tennis ball cut in half
- Plastic drawer tidy
- Yoghurt container
- Plastic plant pots (with the bases taped up)
- Empty crisp or potato chip tube
- Cardboard box or lid lined with a plastic bag

CAUTION: If you are using thin plastic food packaging as a mould, make sure the melted soap base is not too hot as it may melt or warp the plastic.

Ready-made moulds

Moulds specifically designed for making soap are available from many different suppliers (see pages 148–151 for details) or Internet auction sites). Soap-making moulds are usually made with several different moulds on a sheet. As well as plain rectangles or heart shapes, you will also find many fun-themed moulds including animals, shells, stars or novelty items. Moulds made for chocolate-making are also suitable, and some of these are especially good for guest soaps or small soaps that can be embedded in translucent soap base.

The basic soap recipe

Use this basic 'melt-and-pour' vegetable glycerine soap recipe to make all the individual variations on pages 87–147. When you have mastered it you can adapt it to make your own designer soaps.

Ingredients

1 litre or 1kg (35oz) melted soap base
4 teaspoons essential oil or fragrance oil (2%)

Suggested additives (choose one or more)

1–2 tablespoons dried herbs
1 teaspoon clay
1 teaspoon mica or glitter
1–2 teaspoons oil, melted butter or Vitamin E
1 teaspoon honey or beeswax
A few drops of liquid colouring

How much soap base?

To work this out, simply fill your mould with water and pour it into a measuring jug. The amount of water in the jug will be the amount of melted soap you will need: 1 litre (1¾ pints) = approx. 1 kilo (2¼ lbs). If you overestimate, simply pour any excess melted base into a plastic tub to set. 'Melt and pour' soap bases can be re-used several times over.

Tip

*You may prefer to melt sufficient soap for several projects and ladle the liquid soap into the measuring jug as required.
Do not leave the base on the heat for too long as the water will evaporate and the soap will become thick and coloured.*

Making the mixture

Fill the mould with water and pour into a measuring jug (see 'How much soap base?' on facing page).

Using a chopping board or work surface, cut the soap base into 2.5–5cm (1–2in) chunks using a kitchen knife.

Put the soap chunks into a large non-metal measuring jug (for microwave) or heavy-based saucepan (for hob).

Melting the base

Whether using a microwave or a saucepan on a hob, melt the base gently, until it becomes liquid, at approximately 160–165°F (70–75°C), depending on the base used. Do not overheat as the base may burn and become thick, cloudy or caramel coloured. It may also warp thin moulds.

Place the container in the microwave and heat on full power. Start with 20 seconds and continue in 10-second bursts until the base is melted, stirring between bursts. Stirring should disperse small chunks of soap left in the hot base without further heating. Take care not to get any of the hot soap on your skin.

Alternatively, melt the soap base on top of the stove in a heavy-based saucepan or double boiler. Heat gently, stirring, until the soap is almost melted, then turn off heat and stir until the rest of the soap melts.

Tip

If using a microwave, the container should be considerably larger in volume than the soap base it contains to prevent spills.

Adding extra ingredients

Mix any powdered additives with a little water before adding to the base, to prevent clumping. See basic recipe for suitable additives and recommended quantities.

Melt additives like beeswax, hard oil or butters by heating gently in a saucepan or a metal jug on a hob. Stir gently to avoid creating bubbles in the soap. If using a jug with a metal handle (as shown), remember that the handle will be hot.

Combine additives with the soap base. Heavy ingredients may sink to the bottom, so allow the base to cool and thicken slightly before adding ingredients such as pumice, loofah or oats. If the base becomes too thick to pour, melt it down and start again. Additives may affect the colour or scent, so do not add colouring or fragrance at this stage.

Adding fragrance

Soaps may be scented with essential oils (plant essences) or fragrance oils (scents made using synthetic aroma chemicals). The recommended quantity is 10–20g (2–4 teaspoons) of fragrance or essential oil to every kilo of soap base or 1–2% of weight. Do not add more than 3% fragrance or essential oil (30g per kilo of base) as it may irritate the skin. It may also turn the soap cloudy.

Add the fragrance oil or essential oil, mixing in thoroughly to ensure even distribution. Do not add colour at this stage as some essential or fragrance oils contain a hint of colour that may affect the base. For example, adding blue colouring after a brown-tinted fragrance oil would produce a green-blue, rather than a blue soap base.

CAUTION: Use only skin-safe cosmetic fragrances for soap, never potpourri or candle fragrances. Mix in very thoroughly, as any concentrated areas of unmixed fragrance may cause skin irritation.

Adding colour

The easiest way to colour soaps is with cosmetic grade water-based liquid colour. Soap colours are usually very concentrated and half a drop may be all that is needed. Remember that the strength or dilution of liquid colour may vary from supplier to supplier.

Add the liquid colour drop by drop.

Stir in the colour thoroughly, to ensure even distribution.

Pouring and spritzing

Make sure the melted soap base contains all the herbs, glitter, micas, oils, fragrance and colour that you wish to add. Pour into a plastic container or mould, or a container lined with plastic food wrap or bag.

CAUTION: Surgical spirit or alcohol should always be kept away from a naked flame.

After pouring, small bubbles usually appear on the surface of the soap. These will set and spoil its appearance. Spritz or spray the bubbles with surgical spirit or alcohol to make them disappear as if by magic.

Note: if you do not have any surgical spirit, smooth over the bubbles using the back of a spoon.

Tip

Before beginning to pour lots of small soaps, make sure the base is fairly hot or it may begin to set in the jug. Adding a teaspoon of water per litre/kilo (1¾ pints/2¼lbs) of soap will make the base more liquid and allow more pouring time. The excess water will eventually evaporate. Remember that you can always pop it back in the microwave to make it more liquid again.

Cooling and unmoulding

Once you have poured your soap, leave it to cool. The time it will take to set will depend on the pouring temperature of the soap and the thickness of the bar. Small thin soaps or a soap sheet for rolls or swirls may be ready in 10 minutes, while soaps made in a loaf mould or margarine tub are best left to cool for several hours or overnight.

If using a rectangular mould, gently pull the sides away from the sides of the soap, turn upside down and gently press the mould until the soap pops out.

If you are using a shaped mould, turn upside down and gently press all around the top of the mould until the soap is released. Turn the mould upside-down to release the soap.

Cutting the soap

If you have made a loaf mould or large rectangular soap you may wish to cut it into individual bars. Cutting soap is similar to cutting through hard cheese. Any kitchen knife may be used, and it does not have to be particularly sharp.

The soap may also be cut using a soap cutter. These are available from soap making suppliers.

For an attractive effect, use a wavy potato chip cutter to cut the soap.

Further techniques

Melt and pour soap bases are very versatile. Once you have understood and perfected the various techniques, you will be able to create wonderful masterpieces of your own. These techniques will enable you to make all the recipes in this book.

Layering

Different colours of soap may be poured on top of one another to produce attractive layered effect. Pour the first layer and leave to set slightly so a skin forms on top. This must be set enough to hold the weight of the next layer and must still be warm.

Test the top layer with your finger; it should leave an indentation. Spritz or spray the first layer generously with surgical spirit to help the second layer stick or bind. Make sure the soap base is not too hot or it will melt the skin of the first layer and the layers will merge. Colour and pour the next layer. Repeat as required.

Leave soap to set, then cut the block into bars.

Swirling and marbling

To make a marbled soap, swirl two different coloured soaps together. Make sure the soap base is not too hot (i.e. too runny), so the two colours marble together rather than merging into one colour. Pour the melted base into two different jugs, add a different colour to each, then pour both soaps at the same time. For a more marbled effect, use a wooden toothpick to swirl the colours.

Cookie cutter shapes

Line a tray or cardboard box lid with a plastic bag or food wrap. Colour the soap, adding a teaspoon of water to every kilo or litre (2¼lbs or 1¾ pints) of melted base to make it softer and easier to cut. Pour the soap into the container to a depth of approximately 1.5cm (½in), or the desired thickness to make a sheet of soap.

Leave to set until just firm, pressing a finger into the centre of the soap sheet to check consistency. Do not leave until completely cold as it will be harder to cut. Lift the soap sheet out of the container, remove the plastic wrap and place on a chopping board. Cut out your soaps using a cookie cutter.

Remove the soap shape from the cutter and leave to set until hard. Wrap with food wrap or place in a cellophane bag. Any leftover pieces can be melted down and used again.

CAUTION: Make sure the sheet of soap is not too thick or hard before cutting, as it may break or warp the cookie cutter.

Rolls and shapes

Pour the soap into a plastic tray or baking tray lined with plastic food wrap. Add a teaspoon of water to every kilo or litre (2¼lbs or 1¾ pints) of melted soap base to make it more pliable.

Leave to set until only just firm and pliable. If you wish, spritz with alcohol and pour on another thin layer of different-coloured soap to make a two-tone roll. Remove soap from tray. You may wish to cut and trim the edges of the rectangle to leave a clean edge.

Working very quickly, roll up the soap rectangle, or bend it into an 'S' shape. Cut the rectangle in half widthways, if too long.

Leave the soap roll or 'S' shape to set until hard, then spritz thoroughly with surgical spirit. Place in a clean cylindrical potato chip container or loaf mould. Pour in a contrasting colour soap.

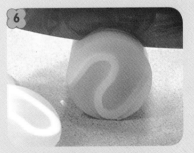

Leave to set, then remove the roll carefully from the chip mould.

Cut the soaps. The overall effect should resemble a stick of seaside rock with the roll embed going right through the centre.

CAUTION: **Make sure the soap is not too hot or it may melt the soap roll embed. The soap should be cool enough for you to be able to leave your hand on the side of the jug containing it.**

Making a scroll

1 Pour the soap into a plastic tray or baking tray lined with food wrap. Add a teaspoon of water to every kilo or litre (2¼lbs or 1¾ pints) of melted soap base to make it more pliable. Leave to set until just firm but still pliable.

2 Make a tie to go round the scroll by cutting each side of the rectangle. Begin at the top, approximately 2cm (¾in) in and finish at the bottom edge so you have two very long triangles of soap.

3 Starting at the widest end of the soap, roll up into a scroll.

4 Cut a small nick in the widest part of one of the long, leftover triangles of soap.

5 Wrap the triangle around the soap and push the narrow end of the long triangle through the nick in the wide end.

The finished scroll

Embedding and decoration

An embed is a small item embedded or buried in the soap, and a wide range of items is suitable. You can use any small soap made in an ice cube tray or small chocolate mould; small chunks of soap; soap swirls or soaps cut out with mini cookie cutters. Other ideas include stamps, coins, photographs, stickers, artwork, transfers, erasers, beads, ribbons or plastic toys.

Make or select suitable embeds. Pour a little soap base into the bottom of the mould and leave for a few minutes for a skin to form.

Test the soap with a finger to make sure a skin has formed.

Spritz the bottom layer of soap with surgical spirit and place the embed on top, then spritz the embed. The surgical spirit helps to bind the soap layers and the embed.

Pour the next layer of soap on top. Take care that it is not too hot or the embed may melt. If you can leave your hand on the side of the jug, the soap base should be cool enough to pour.

Tip

If you want to use photographs or paper images, first laminate them or cover in clear PVC packing tape. This will make the image waterproof and prevent it from bleeding into the soap.

Alternative method

Fill the mould with melted soap and leave to set until a skin has formed on top and the soap in the mould has begun to thicken. Using the point of a knife or a toothpick, break the surface of the soap, spritz the embed and push it into the soap.

CAUTION: Make sure any small parts used for embeds are kept away from small children and animals.

Decoration

Soaps may be decorated by gently pressing in flowers or dried fruit when the soap it is just starting to set.

Storing soaps

If melt and pour vegetable glycerine soaps are left unwrapped in a cold or humid environment, the glycerine in them will attract moisture and leave the soaps wet and slimy. To prevent this, wrap the finished bars in plastic food wrap or cellophane.

Do not leave soaps in direct light as their colour will fade very quickly, particularly if you have used powdered herbs to colour them. Soaps should be good to use for up to a year after making, sometimes even longer depending on the ingredients used.

Health and safety

Remember that melted soap is hot and can burn if it comes in contact with the skin. The skin and eyes must also be protected from neat essential oils. You may therefore wish to use protective clothing, gloves and goggles while making soap. If soap or any of the ingredients that you are using come in contact with the eyes, irrigate immediately with water. Label all ingredients and finished products clearly and keep well away from children and pets.

Reheating soap

Soap bases may be melted down several times, though some of the water content will evaporate each time. To prevent it becoming dry and brittle, add 1 teaspoon of water to each kilo or litre (2¼lbs or 1¾ pints) of soap that you wish to re-melt. If soap that you are re-melting is fragranced, take care to allow for this before adding more fragrance. Too much may irritate the skin, and it is recommended that the finished soap should contain 1–2% of fragrance in total.

Selling

The information in this book is to enable you to produce soaps for home use. If you want to manufacture products for sale, you should investigate fully the appropriate trading legislation of your country and of countries to whom you wish to sell. Most countries have strict legislation on weights and measures, manufacturers' details, batch numbers, record keeping, health and safety and insurances etc. In Europe bath products must also be certificated by a Cosmetic Chemist.

If you are giving soaps to a friend or family member, it is wise to label with the ingredients and store soaps and ingredients away from children and pets.

Troubleshooting: hints and suggestions

Making soap with melt and pour bases is relatively simple and problem-free. The following hints should help you to overcome the few problems that may arise

Layers are not sticking together

Make sure you spritz the surface of the soap between each layer using surgical spirit or alcohol. Do not let a layer cool down too much before adding the next. When pouring another layer, the layer below should be warm with a skin on the surface of the soap.

Soaps will not unmould

Make sure soaps are completely cold and set before attempting to unmould them. If they will not come out, they may not be set. Leave them for a couple of hours or overnight, then try again. If you are in a hurry, place them in a refrigerator for a few minutes to speed up the setting process. Alternatively, slide the mould carefully along to a cooler part of the kitchen surface or table.

Soap embeds melting

Make sure the base is not too hot when pouring it on to a soap embed. Check also that the soap embeds are not too thin, or they may melt with the heat of the poured soap.

Embeds falling out of soap

Make sure that you spritz the soap embed fully and that the soap base you are pouring on to the embed is not too cool; experiment with different temperatures of soap.

Cloudy soaps

The soap base may have been overheated, heated too many times, or you may have added too much fragrance. Some 'natural' soap bases are slightly cloudy rather than crystal clear; if in doubt consult your supplier before ordering.

Bleeding colour

Most liquid colours will bleed into each other over time. To prevent this, non-bleeding colours are available from some suppliers.

Sweaty soap

The vegetable glycerine in melt and pour soap attracts moisture from the air, which in cold, damp or humid conditions can make it sweaty and wet. As soon as the soap has hardened and is dry to the touch, wrap it in food wrap or place in a cellophane bag.

Spots on soap

If little white dots appear on your soaps, the sugar crystals in the base may not have dissolved completely. This happens when the soap has not been heated to the required temperature. Some bases, particularly 'natural' types, have slightly higher melting temperatures, so check with the manufacturer when purchasing. Another reason may be that the soaps have been wrapped while damp: make sure soaps are dry to the touch before wrapping.

Discoloured soap base

If you overheat the soap base it may change to a brown or caramel colour with an unpleasant smell. Melt the soap base gently, and do not leave on the heat for long periods. The soap base may in theory be melted down several times, but for best results try to use it on the first or second time of melting.

Additives sinking to the bottom

Heavy additives such as pumice, oats or loofah may sink to the bottom of the soap if the base is too hot when pouring. Before pouring a base that contains heavy additives, stir it continually to cool and thicken it, as this will help to suspend the additives.

Basic ingredients

Essential oils

What are essential oils?

Essential oils are the spirit, personality or essence of an aromatic plant. They are the fragrant, natural volatile liquids found in plants, leaves, fruit, seeds, roots, wood, resin, gum, grasses and flowers. On a hot day, plants release them into the air, either as protection from pests and infection or to attract bees and insects for pollination. Some essential oils are used commercially to repel or attract insects. Essential oils are antiseptic, and some are also antiviral, antifungal and antibacterial. They are widely used in aromatherapy to help to ease a multitude of complaints and conditions. At the same time they affect mood and well-being, helping to relax both the body and mind.

Aromatherapy

Aromatherapy is a non-medical complementary holistic practice of caring for the body. Treatments involve the inhalation or topical application of aromatic plant oils, which have been used for centuries for their antiseptic, antiviral, antifungal and antibacterial properties to control infections. Essential oils are applied in several ways including massage, inhalation, vaporisation, compresses, bath products and skincare, to help ease common ailments, aid relaxation and stress and to improve physical, mental and emotional health.

The term 'aromathérapie' was coined in the 1920s by a French chemist and means literally a therapy using aromas. René-Maurice Gattefossé is reputed to have discovered the healing and antiseptic properties of essential oils when he burned his arm and grabbed lavender oil, the nearest available substance, to cool it.

The pain relief and speedy healing that followed prompted him to spend his life researching the subject. In 1964 another Frenchman, Dr Jean Valnet, carried out further research on wounded soldiers and published his well-known aromatherapists' bible *The Practice of Aromatherapy*.

The olfactory sense is one of the first to develop and a smell can instantly remind us of a childhood memory or place from the past. Aromas can also trigger a change in mood: imagine how a stroll in a fragrant rose garden can lift and calm the spirits, while a walk down a garbage-strewn alleyway promotes an unpleasant feeling, thereby lowering the spirits. The aroma of essential oils is believed to have the same effect on mood: simply by breathing in the floral aroma of lavender we may feel relaxed, calm and de-stressed, while the scent of lemons can awaken our senses and invigorate and refresh the mind.

A warm bath is one of the most pleasurable ways to use essential oils, as the complex chemical compounds they contain are believed to enter the bloodstream through the skin. The blissful sensation of surrounding your body with aromatic scents is one of the most effective ways of unwinding and letting go of the day's tensions and stresses.

Some therapeutic uses of essential oils

Dry skin — chamomile, geranium, neroli, palmarosa, patchouli, rose geranium, sandalwood and ylang ylang.

Ageing and mature skin — bog myrtle, frankincense, geranium, myrrh, neroli, palmarosa, patchouli, lavender, rose geranium and sandalwood

Oily skin — bergamot, bog myrtle, cypress, cedarwood, geranium, juniper, lavender, lemon, lime, mandarin, neroli, orange, rose geranium and sandalwood,

Sensitive skin — bog myrtle, chamomile, lavender, neroli and sandalwood

Fungal infections such as athlete's foot or ringworm — bog myrtle, lemon, manuka, myrrh, pine and tea tree

Eczema or dermatitis — bergamot, cedarwood, chamomile, geranium, lavender and sandalwood

Stretchmarks and scars — frankincense, geranium, lavender, neroli, patchouli, mandarin and elemi.

PMT and painful periods — clary sage, chamomile, cypress, frankincense, geranium, grapefruit, jasmine, lavender, rose geranium, neroli, marjoram and yarrow

Muscle aches — black pepper, coriander, cypress, eucalyptus, ginger, grapefruit, juniper, lavender, marjoram, pine, rosemary, vetiver and yarrow.

Anxiety, depression or stress — bog myrtle, bergamot, chamomile, clary sage, cypress, frankincense, jasmine, lavender, mandarin, marjoram, neroli, orange, palmarosa, vetiver and ylang ylang

CAUTION: Essential oils are known to have different therapeutic benefits and are reported to have been of great help in easing various skin conditions. Oils must not be used directly on the skin and should be used in a carrier oil, bath bomb, soap or cream.

How are essential oils obtained?

It can take a huge amount of raw material to obtain even a small amount of precious essential oil, so large areas of crops are needed. Different extraction methods are used to obtain the essential oils of plants which are held in special cells within the plant tissues. The oils move around the plant during different times of the year or day so must be picked for oil extraction at the optimum time for that particular plant. The oils and perfumes from aromatic plants are very delicate and should be removed gently to retain the life force and unique properties of each.

Steam distillation

This is the most common form of extraction and creates floral waters as a by-product. Steam releases the essential oil into water vapour which is passed along a pipe to a condenser, then cooled back into water. The oil floats to the surface and is skimmed off, filtered and packaged.

Expression

Essential oil from citrus fruit is stored in the large cells in the coloured outer rind, or peel, close to the surface of the fruit. The fruit is pressed either by hand or by machine to release the essential oil.

Solvent extraction

Some flowers, including jasmine, mimosa, hyacinth and tuberose, are too delicate to be steam distilled. Essential oil is extracted by pouring a solvent over the fragile flowers, which penetrates the plant tissue and dissolves the oil into the solvent. This concentrated oily substance known as a 'concrete' is then purified into an 'absolute'. Solvent extraction produces a substance with an aroma closer to the original plant than essential oil, so absolutes are widely used in perfume manufacture.

Enfleurage

Before the development of solvent extraction, freshly picked flowers and purified fat were layered and left to infuse on glass plates. After a few days, the flowers were replaced, and over time the fat became saturated with essential oil. The resulting 'pomade' was mixed with alcohol to separate the essential oil from the fat. The fragrant fat was often used in the manufacture of soap.

Gas extraction

The latest extraction method uses a gas such as carbon dioxide or nitrogen under very high pressure. The resulting oil is high in quality, with no remaining solvents.

Safety

Essential oils should not be taken internally and must be kept away from children and animals. If oils are accidentally swallowed, seek medical advice immediately. If essential oils come in contact with the eyes, irrigate with water immediately and seek medical advice. Though essential oils have been used historically to ease medical conditions, they are no substitute for medical advice.

Essential oils are very potent and bath products contain only small amounts. Most should not be used undiluted on the body. Do not exceed the amounts stated in the recipes.

Unless otherwise specified, the recipes in this book are intended for those over the age of seven. Most essential oils should not be used by young children; the exceptions are lavender, geranium, chamomile, mandarin and yarrow, and these at no more that 0.5%. However, you can adapt them for use by young children by reducing the amount of fragrance or essential oils. If you suffer from allergies, carry out a skin test patch before using your soap.

Essential oils from some citrus fruits may cause a reaction when combined with sunlight. Avoid direct exposure to sunlight or ultraviolet (UV) light for approximately 12 hours after using orange, lemon, grapefruit, bergamot, petitgrain, lime and mandarin oils. They may also damage clothing and wooden surfaces, so cover yourself and your surfaces before using them.

Seek advice from a qualified practitioner or medical adviser if you:

- have a known medical condition such as high blood pressure or epilepsy
- are receiving any psychiatric or medical treatment
- taking homeopathic or herbal remedies
- pregnant or breast-feeding
- wish to treat young children

Storage

Essential oils should be stored in dark coloured glass jars or bottles in a cool environment. Many oils can last for years if stored in this way, though citrus oils will generally lose their properties after approximately a year. Exposure to oxygen will quickly degrade essential oils and perfumes, so make sure there is as little space between the oil surface and the top of the bottle as possible.

Directory of essential oils

There are too many essential oils to list in this book, so here is a selection of the most common and readily available oils with brief descriptions of each. The letter after the name of each denotes whether it is a top **(T)**, middle **(M)** or base note **(B)**. **(T, M)** indicates a top to middle note that may be used as either. The perfumery technique section (see pages 52–61) contains information on top, middle and base notes and how to blend your own therapeutic perfume for use in your soaps.

Bergamot (T)
Citrus bergamia

Fragrance: sweet, fresh, green, bright citrusy scent with a warm floral quality.

Known uses: lifting the spirits, stress, depression, boosting immunity, colds and flu, thrush, urinary tract infection. Bergamot is a small, bitter orange from Lombardy, Italy. It is best known for its flavouring of Earl Grey tea and is one of the main ingredients in eau de Cologne. Strongly phototoxic so use sparingly, maximum usage 0.4%.

Blends with: jasmine, cypress, neroli, lavender, black pepper, clary sage, frankincense, geranium, mandarin, nutmeg, orange, rosemary, sandalwood, vetiver and ylang ylang.

Black Pepper (M)
Piper nigrum

Fragrance: fresh, warm, musty, sharp, spicy and dry-woody smell.

Known uses: digestion, colds and flu, immune system, circulation, cellulite, aches, pains, rheumatism, relaxing muscles, aphrodisiac. One of the oldest known spices, it is known to have been used in India more than 4,000 years ago. Concentrations of more than 0.5% are not recommended.

Blends with: sandalwood, frankincense, juniper, rosemary, cardamom, fennel, cedarwood, ginger, bergamot, neroli, bergamot, clary sage, clove, coriander, geranium, grapefruit, lavender, lemon, lime, mandarin, sage, and ylang-ylang.

Bog Myrtle (T)
Myrica gale

Fragrance: clear, fresh, sweet, camphoraceous, herbaceous scent, slightly menthol.

Known uses: particularly useful as an insect repellent and can be used in place of Citronella. Also known as Sweet Gale, it is native to Northern Europe and North America and has properties similar to tea tree oil. It is enjoying a revival in skincare products for its anti-ageing properties and its use for sensitive skin, oily skin, open pores and acne. Historically, it has also been used for depression, poor memory, to promote well-being and, before the use of hops, to flavour beer.

Blends with: other resinous oils, lemon, juniper, lime, cypress, lavender, tea tree.

Cardamom (M)
Elettaria cardamomum

Fragrance: warm, fruity, sweet and spicy aromatic scent with a pungent freshness and woody, floral undertones.

Known uses: digestion, nausea, heartburn, coughs, flatulence, bad breath caused by gastric problems, mental fatigue, aphrodisiac, and a general tonic. Botanically related to ginger, it has been used in traditional Chinese and Ayurvedic medicine for more than 3,000 years and is used today in Eastern medicinal practice as a tonic for the lungs and for its immune-boosting properties.

Blends with: rosemary, frankincense, sandalwood, ylang ylang, bergamot, cinnamon, clove, caraway and cedarwood.

Cedarwood (B)

Cedrus atlantica or *Juniperus virginiana*

Fragrance: clean-smelling, sharp and fresh with slightly sweet, woody, balsamic undertones.

Known uses: acne, arthritis, rheumatism, bronchitis, nervous tension, eczema, oily skin, cystitis and urinary infections. A native tree of North America, the oil is distilled from wood chips and sawdust and was used historically in medicine by the Native Americans. The ancient Egyptians are known to have used it as an insect repellent and in mummification.

Blends with: bergamot, cinnamon, cypress, frankincense, jasmine, juniper, lavender, lemon, neroli, myrrh, sandalwood, vetiver and rosemary.

Chamomile (Roman) (M)

Anthemis nobilis

Fragrance: Refreshing, sweet, herbaceous, apple-like, fresh scent.

Known uses: Widely used in babies' and children's products. Anti-inflammatory, menstrual cramps, insomnia, migraine, PMS, restlessness, stress, allergies. This soothing and calming oil is pale blue in colour and said to be beneficial to those with hay fever (unless you have an allergy to ragweed). Also known as ground apple.

Blends with: clary sage, bergamot, lavender, geranium, jasmine, tea tree, grapefruit, lemon, ylang-ylang, marjoram, rose geranium and mandarin.

Clary Sage (T, M)

Salvia sclarea

Fragrance: Sweet, nutty, rich, herbaceous.

Known uses: Muscle relaxant, depression, menstrual cramps, stress, nervous tension, insomnia, aphrodisiac. Do not use during pregnancy or when drinking alcohol as it can make you drowsy.

Blends with: juniper, lavender, sandalwood, coriander, geranium, jasmine, lemon, pine, frankincense and citrus oils.

Cypress (M)

Cupressus sempervirens

Fragrance: earthy, fresh and green, smoky and nutty with a slight spiciness and sweet, resinous notes.

Known uses: spasmodic coughs, bronchitis, lymphatic drainage, detoxifying, cellulite, water retention, soothes emotions, varicose veins, haemorrhoids, circulation and chilblains. Historically used as an incense ingredient and in aftershaves and colognes.

Blends with: juniper, pine, bergamot, clary sage, lavender, marjoram, sandalwood, rosemary, frankincense and all the citrus oils.

Clary sage

Cardamom pods

Dried chamomile flowers

Elemi (M)

Canarium luzonicum

Fragrance: fresh, citrusy, peppery, balsamic, rich, sweet and spicy.

Known uses: Bronchitis, catarrh, phlegm, healing of scars, immune system, emotional healing, harmonising, calming, mature, rough dry wrinkly skin, skin and nail fungus, skin disorders. A resinous gum with a pleasant aroma, used by the ancient Egyptians for embalming.

Blends with: all citrus oils, cinnamon, clove, frankincense, lavender, myrrh, rosemary and sage.

Eucalyptus (T)

Eucalyptus globulus

Fragrance: strong medicinal, sharp, fresh, camphoraceous smell with slight woody undertones.

Known uses: not used much in perfumery but historically used as a medicinal herb by Australian Aborigines. Fevers, colds, bronchitis, rheumatism, muscular aches and pains, urinary and genital infections. **Caution: must not be swallowed.**

Blends with: cypress, lavender, marjoram, cedarwood, lemongrass, tea tree, lemon, thyme and pine.

Eucalyptus

Fennel (T, M)

Foeniculum vulgare

Fragrance: Spicy-sweet, green, herby aniseed-like scent.

Known uses: digestion, nausea, vomiting, colitis, diuretic, kidney stones, flatulence, constipation, nervous indigestion, bloatedness, obesity, coughs and bronchitis. Well used in ancient times, it was cultivated by the Romans for courage and strength. In medieval times it was known as 'fenkle' and used to ward off evil spirits. The modern name fennel comes from the Latin *foenum*, or hay. Avoid during pregnancy or if you have epilepsy, and do not use in high concentrations.

Blends with: geranium, lavender, marjoram and sandalwood.

Frankincense (B)

Boswellia carterii

Fragrance: base note with sweet, woody, resinous undertones.

Known uses: meditation, stress, anti-inflammatory, damaged or ageing skin, toning, rejuvenating, anxiety, tension, mucus conditions (i.e. coughs, bronchitis, laryngitis). A highly prized gum resin, used as far back as the ancient Egyptians for skin-care and in incense for worship and fumigation of the sick.

Blends with: neroli, pine, sandalwood, myrrh, cedarwood, vetiver, sandalwood, lavender, orange, bergamot and lemon.

Geranium (T, M)

Pelargonium graveolens

Fragrance: fresh, rosy, sweet floral with a hint of lemon and fresh green.

Known uses: neuralgia, anxiety, depression, sedative, uplifting, diuretic, dry and inflamed skin, hot flushes, oily skin, skin toner and tonic. Widely used in perfumery, and can be used in skincare, and in baby products at 0.5%.

Blends with: any oil, particularly bergamot, marjoram, palmarosa, sandalwood, cedarwood, clary sage, grapefruit, jasmine, lavender, lime, neroli, orange and rosemary.

Ginger (T, M)

Zingiber officinale

Fragrance: hot, dry, pungent and musty, with a lingering spicy sweetness.

Known uses: colds and flu, fevers, immune system, poor circulation, muscular pains, nausea, aphrodisiac. Ginger root has been traditionally used in Chinese medicine for digestion and circulation.

Blends with: all citrus and spicy oils, particularly bergamot, frankincense, neroli, sandalwood, ylang ylang, vetiver, juniper, and cedarwood.

Grapefruit (T)

Citrus grandis

Fragrance: fresh, green, zesty, sweet and citrus smell.

Known uses: detoxifying, tonic, oily skin, acne, cellulite, insomnia, constipation, digestive, liver and kidney problems, hangovers, immune system, colds and influenza. A good pick-me-up with a positive effect on the mind and helpful for sufferers of seasonal affective disorder (SAD).

Blends with: bergamot, palmarosa, frankincense, geranium, eucalyptus and pine.

Hyssop (T, M)

Hyssopus officinalis

Fragrance: sweet camphoraceous top note with a spicy, herbaceous and warming undertone.

Known uses: respiratory problems, colds, flu, coughs, sore throats, bronchitis, asthma, tonsillitis and catarrh. It is said to help the digestion, flatulence, indigestion and colic, alertness, fatigue, rheumatism, bruises, grief, spleen. It can regulate blood pressure, reduce water-retention during menstruation and is used as a tonic for convalescents. Hyssop is an ingredient in the ancient herbal liqueur Chartreuse, made by Carthusian monks at France's Grande Chartreuse monastery. Do not use if epileptic or during pregnancy.

Blends with: geranium, orange, clary sage, melissa and rosemary.

Jasmine (M, B)

Jasminum officinale

Fragrance: rich, warm, sweet, exotic floral scent.

Known uses: anxiety, depression, dry and sensitive skin, aphrodisiac, labour pains, post-natal depression, menstrual pain. The name derives from the Arabic yasmin. Because of its importance in the perfume industry, it is known as 'the king of oils'. The day-old flowers are picked at night.

Blends with: bergamot, sandalwood and all citrus oils.

Ginger root

Grapefruit

Jasmine

Juniper (M)

Juniperus communis

Fragrance: fresh, warm, pungent, camphoraceous, woody, herbaceous smell.

Known uses: detox, digestion, urinary tract, diuretic, respiratory complaints, concentration, rheumatism, gout, circulation, oily skin, acne. Juniper berries are used in the production of gin.

Blends with: cedarwood, bergamot, cypress, ginger, sandalwood, lavender, pine, rosemary and all citrus oils.

Lavender (T, M)

Lavandula angustifolia

Fragrance: fresh, light, soft, clean sweet and floral.

Known uses: an extremely useful oil and the most widely used for its therapeutic benefits which are too numerous to list. The most common uses are stress, nervous tension, pain, insomnia, headaches, neuralgia, eczema, psoriasis, thrush, wounds, burns, stings, bites, shock, repelling insects. The Romans used lavender to bathe and its name is derived from 'lavare', their name for bathing. Widely used in perfumery, it blends well with many other essential oils, and as the most versatile, it must be the number one choice for every first aid kit. Can be used at 0.5% in baby products.

Blends with: all oils.

Lemon (T)

Citrus medica limonum

Fragrance: fresh, sweet, green, citrus smell.

Known uses: tonic, detox, diuretic, digestion, colds, flu, arthritis, immune system, lymphatic drainage, concentration, oily skin, rheumatism, arthritis, gout, abscesses, boils, acne, high blood pressure, varicose veins, circulation. The name 'limonum' is thought to have derived from the Arabic 'limun' and the Persian 'lumum'. Lemon is a rich source of vitamin C and was given to sailors on long journeys to prevent scurvy and other mineral deficiencies.

Blends with: lavender, sandalwood, benzoin, eucalyptus, geranium, fennel, juniper and neroli.

Lemongrass (T, M)

Cymbopogon schoenanthus or *Cymbopogon citratus*

Fragrance: citrus, herbaceous, fresh, sweet, zesty lemon scent.

Known uses: tonic, digestion, migraine, respiratory conditions, fever, muscular aches and pains, constipation, depression, anxiety, nervous exhaustion, stress, athlete's foot, acne, jet-lag, as a pick-me-up, hangovers, repelling insects such as fleas, ticks and lice in pets. A fast-growing perennial grass from India, it is known locally as 'choomana poolu' and is used in Ayurvedic medicine to help cool fevers and to treat infectious diseases. **Caution: phototoxic**.

Blends with: geranium, tea tree, vetiver, cedarwood, jasmine, lavender, pine, eucalyptus, neroli, palmarosa and rosemary.

Lavender

Lime (T)

Citrus aurantifolia

Fragrance: fresh, green, sharp, and zesty citrus peel aroma.

Known uses: astringent, tonic, headaches, fevers, immune system, flu, bronchitis, sinusitis, clearing the mind, oily skin, acne, depression, circulation, cellulite, obesity, travel sickness, arthritis and rheumatism.

Blends with: juniper, neroli, lavender, clary sage, ylang ylang and citrus oils.

Mandarin (T)

Citrus nobilis

Fragrance: very sweet, rich, tangy, zesty and floral scent.

Known uses: restless children with tantrums, stress, stretchmarks, nervous indigestion, oily skin, digestion, stomach cramps, flatulence, diarrhoea, constipation, circulation, fluid retention, insomnia. One of the gentlest oils, mandarin may be used by children, during pregnancy and for the elderly at 0.5%. May be slightly phototoxic.

Blends with: chamomile, lavender, frankincense, juniper, bergamot, clary sage, lavender, nutmeg and neroli.

Manuka (T, M)

Leptospermum scoparium

Fragrance: a sweet honey-like aroma, with woody, mossy notes.

Known uses: highly bactericidal and insecticidal with a wide variety of uses including cuts, spots, boils, ulcers, stress, anxiety, nervous tension and dry and sensitive skin. Its effect is so powerful that Manuka honey has been introduced into hospitals to fight 'superbugs'. Research suggests anti-bacterial, anti-fungal, and anti-inflammatory properties similar to tea tree, but up to 20 times more effective and less sensitizing. Its aroma is also more pleasing. Though relatively new to the modern practice of aromatherapy, it has been used historically as a medicinal herb by the Maori in New Zealand.

Blends with: bergamot, black pepper, cedarwood, ginger, juniper, lavender, peppermint, rosemary, sandalwood, vetiver and ylang ylang.

Marjoram (M)

Origanum marjorana

Fragrance: warm, woody, slightly spicy, soft and sweet aroma.

Known uses: muscular aches, insomnia, sedative, digestion, pre-menstrual tension (PMT), hypertension, rheumatism, arthritis, colds, bronchitis, migraine, nervous indigestion. The name 'origanum' comes from the Greek meaning 'joy of the mountains'.

Blends with: lavender, bergamot, ginger, vetiver, cypress, cedarwood, chamomile, eucalyptus and tea tree.

Marjoram

Lime

Mandarin

Myrrh (B)

Commiphora myrrha

Fragrance: dry, warm, musty, balsamic with rich, spicy sweet notes.

Known uses: gum disease, coughs, gingivitis, ageing skin, skin infections, fungal infections, mouth ulcers, chapped skin, eczema, boils, skin ulcers, bedsores, chapped and cracked skin, ringworm, weeping wounds, gangrene, athlete's foot, stress, anxiety and expelling mucus and phlegm. It is a gum resin prized since ancient times for its healing properties. The Egyptians used it for embalming and in skincare to preserve the skin; the Greeks took it to battle to heal wounds. A sacred and spiritual oil, it has been used for centuries as an incense ingredient.

Blends with: frankincense, cypress, lavender, cedarwood and sandalwood.

Neroli (Orange Blossom) (T, M)

Citrus aurantium

Fragrance: exquisite floral, sweet citrus-like scent with rich, soft green undertones. Light and refreshing.

Known uses: tones and rejuvenates the complexion, particularly dry, mature skin, wrinkles and stretchmarks. Helps scar tissue, wounds, cuts, eases nervous indigestion and irritable bowel syndrome (IBS). Uplifting, relaxing, eases panic, insomnia, vertigo, shock and sudden emotional upsets.

Blends with: citrus oils, clary sage, jasmine, lavender, geranium, sandalwood, rosemary and ylang ylang.

Orange (Sweet) (T)

Citrus aurantium dulcis or sinensis

Fragrance: sweet, fresh, fruity smell.

Known uses: slow digestion, liver, constipation, tonic, digestion, nervous indigestion, depression, tension headaches, cellulite, detoxing, obesity, constipation, stress, colds, influenza and immune system. A happy and warming oil.

Blends with: fennel, peppermint, black pepper, ginger, frankincense, sandalwood, vetiver and lavender.

Palmarosa (M)

Cymbopogon martini

Fragrance: soft, sweet, rose-like, floral with gentle notes of lemon.

Known uses: stress, anxiety, nervous tension, calming, uplifting, improving appetite, antiseptic, acne, eczema, urinary tract, diarrhoea, skin care. An aromatic grass with a fragrance similar to rose but much less expensive, it is thus widely used in perfumery.

Blends with: bergamot, geranium, sandalwood, orange, grapefruit, chamomile, rosemary, lime and ylang ylang.

Patchouli (B)

Pogostemon cablin

Fragrance: aromatic, woody and musky with spicy, musty, earthy-sweet undertones.

Known uses: depression, scars, stretchmarks, acne, skin conditioner for dry, cracked or ageing skin, eczema, antiseptic, aphrodisiac. Historically used to protect the fabric of Indian shawls and linen from moths.

Blends with: bergamot, rose geranium, clary sage, geranium, lavender, chamomile, cedarwood and myrrh.

Peppermint (T)

Mentha piperita

Fragrance: strong, fresh, minty aroma with sweet undertones.

Known uses: indigestion, nausea, stomach cramps, headache and migraine, concentration, muscle pains, colds, coughs, deodorant.

Blends with: rosemary, black pepper, ginger, eucalyptus, lavender, marjoram, lemon and rosemary.

Petitgrain (T, M)

Citrus aurantium

Fragrance: fresh, green, floral smell with a hint of citrus and woody undertones.

Known uses: stress, panic, nervous exhaustion, depression, digestion, stomach cramps, muscle spasms, calming, insomnia, greasy skin. Useful for convalescence, emotional conditions, and as a general pick-me-up. petitgrain is distilled from the leaves and twigs of the bitter orange tree, while neroli is obtained from the flower of the same tree, and orange from the fruit

Blends with: juniper, clary sage, clove, lavender, rosemary, bergamot, orange, lemon, neroli, jasmine, palmarosa, sandalwood, chamomile, geranium and ylang ylang.

Pine (M)

Pinus sylvestris

Fragrance: fresh, forest smell with sweet, balsamic tones.

Known uses: urinary infections, as a diuretic, tonic, colds, flu, bronchitis, rheumatism, cystitis, muscular aches and pains, period pains, deodorising and antiseptic.

Blends with: cedarwood, cypress, lemon, eucalyptus, marjoram, juniper, lavender and rosemary.

Rosemary (T, M)

Rosmarinus officinalis

Fragrance: strong, fresh, herbaceous, camphoraceous scent.

Known uses: muscular aches and pains, rheumatism, painful periods, circulation, headaches, concentration, sprains, lymphatic drainage, digestion, colds and flu. Used in incense, sick rooms and to drive away evil spirits.

Blends with: cedarwood, geranium, bergamot, lavender, lemongrass and peppermint.

Pine

Rosemary

Rose Geranium (T, M)

Pelargonium graveolens and *Pelargonium rosa*

Fragrance: fresh, crisp, sweet rosy scent.

Known uses: nervous system, pre-menstrual tension (PMT), anxiety, menopausal symptoms, stress, eczema, lymphatic system, jaundice, haemorrhoids, gallstones and mild depression.

Blends with: bergamot, lime, cedarwood, clary sage, grapefruit, lavender, jasmine, lemon, neroli, rosemary and orange.

Sandalwood (B)

Santalum album

Fragrance: soft, deep, rich, sweet, exotic and woody aroma.

Known uses: urinary and venereal infections, antiseptic, meditation, aphrodisiac, nervous exhaustion, eczema, chest infections, bronchitis, asthma, coughs and dry skin. Used since ancient times for incense, embalming and widely used in the perfume and cosmetics industry.

Blends with: bergamot, palmarosa, geranium, vetiver, ylang ylang, lavender, jasmine, cedarwood, black pepper and myrrh.

Rose geranium

Tea Tree (M)

Melaleuca alternifolia

Fragrance: a fresh, strong, spicy, pungent camphoraceous smell.

Known uses: immune system, colds, influenza, anti-viral, anti-bacterial, anti-fungal, muscle aches and pains, shock, skin infections, genital infections, vaginal thrush, cystitis, herpes, bronchitis, asthma, coughs, sinusitis, tuberculosis, abscesses, acne, burns, oily skin, athlete's foot, ringworm, cold sores, blemishes, warts, sunburn. Native to Australia, tea tree has been used historically by the Aborigines as an antiseptic and for a variety of other medicinal purposes.

Blends with: clove, lavender, eucalyptus, rosemary, pine, lemon and thyme.

Thyme (M)

Thymus vulgaris

Fragrance: warm, sweet, spicy herbaceous scent.

Known uses: anti-bacterial, anti-fungal, anti-viral. Venereal infection, urinary infection, cystitis, colds, flu, coughs, bronchitis, respiratory infection, spasmodic coughs, asthma, digestive system, muscle stiffness, aches, pains, rheumatism, arthritis, acne, boils, body lice, scabies, nerve tonic. Used throughout the ancient world for embalming and incense, it was probably introduced to Europe by the Romans for the purification of rooms and in cooking. In the Middle Ages it was presented to knights to give courage. This potent oil should not be used if pregnant, with high blood pressure or on sensitive or damaged skin.

Blends with: clove, bergamot, grapefruit, eucalyptus, lemon, rosemary, geranium, lavender, lemon and pine.

Vetiver (B)

Vetiveria zizanoides

Fragrance: heavy, sweet, earthy, warm, powerful, smoky scent with a woody, musty undertone.

Known uses: anti-depressant, aphrodisiac, insomnia, stress, circulation, anaemia, rheumatism, arthritis, muscular aches and pains, menstrual cramps, acne, wrinkles, stretch marks, mental and physical exhaustion. Vetiver is known as the 'oil of tranquility' because of its deeply calming and relaxing properties.

Blends with: clary sage, lavender, jasmine, sandalwood, patchouli and ylang ylang.

Yarrow (T)

Achillea millefolium

Fragrance: Penetrating fresh green, sweet herbaceous aroma.

Known uses: effective as a painkiller, antispasmodic and anti-inflammatory, for rheumatoid arthritis, skin disorders, sores, rashes, wounds, haemorrhoids, kidney, bladder, colon, fatigue, insomnia, stress, circulation, muscular aches and pains. Can be used in baby products at up to 0.5%.

Blends with: clary sage, rosemary, chamomile, lavender, geranium, rose geranium, lemon, grapefruit, peppermint, cypress, sandalwood, cedarwood, fennel, palmarosa, ylang ylang, frankincense, lemongrass, ginger, marjoram and vetiver.

Ylang Ylang (M)

Cananga odorata

Fragrance: intensely sweet, powerful, exotic, highly fragrant, floral scent with a creamy middle note.

Known uses: stress, panic attacks, depression, anxiety, nervous conditions, aphrodisiac, high blood pressure, abnormally rapid breathing and heartbeat, impotence and frigidity, oily skin. The name means 'flower of flowers', and it is spread on the beds of newlyweds in Indonesia. Use in moderation: just one or two drops may be enough as too much can bring on a headache or nausea. The distillation process produces different grades of the oil: the first is called ylang ylang 'extra', has the sweetest odour and is used only for the perfume industry. The oil used in aromatherapy is a blend of the other grades of oil.

Blends with: sandalwood, jasmine, grapefruit, lavender, bergamot, cedarwood, jasmine, clary sage, lemon, vetiver and sandalwood.

CAUTION: We have not included rose oil in this section, as it is now considered to be a skin sensitizer and its use in commercial products is heavily restricted to a maximum of 0.1% (0.1g per 100g of soap base = approx. 1–2 drops). Instead of rose oil, use a combination of rose geranium and palmarosa, or a rose fragrance oil.

Perfume and fragrance

The history of perfume

For thousands of years, perfume has been an important part of life and ritual. Its use was recorded by the ancient Egyptians, who were known to have used many fragranced preparations in their daily life.

Scented flowers, woods and plants such as frankincense, myrrh, almond and saffron were added to oil or fat and left to infuse in vases and pots. These aromatic oils were burned as incense during worship, used for animal sacrifices and for embalming the dead; at festivals where guests' heads were anointed with oils; and for coronation ceremonies.

Egyptian society ladies used the most expensive perfumed oils for fashion and allurement, to bathe and moisturize their sun-parched skin. Queen Cleopatra was reputed to have used aromatic perfumes in abundance, not just for bathing, but also for seduction. She adorned her ships with garlands of scented flowers and scented them with perfumes so the sea breeze trailed her sensual aroma, and Mark Antony was captivated.

The use of aromatic oils eventually spread to Greece and Rome and then to Arabia where precious perfumes were a sign of wealth and status and were used in the most important of ceremonies.

As the Roman Empire grew the Romans were increasingly influenced by the customs of the countries they conquered, adopting the use of incense for sacrifice, worship and burial. It was perhaps when they took up the trend of shaving their beards that they began anointing their skin with perfumed fats, oils and powders. These were fragranced with expensive Italian flower essences or ingredients imported from Egypt and Arabia. Saffron, rose, quince flowers, lilies, spikenard, myrrh, narcissus, honey and cinnamon were popular, and unguents made with these scents were applied to the hair, body and feet. These pungent aromas were also used in their banqueting houses, homes, flags and on the sails of ships.

In the past, perfumery not only used botanicals but also some important base notes originally derived from animals. The male musk deer from China and Tibet foraged on aromatic herbs in the high mountain ranges and produced an extremely pungent secretion under its belly called musk.

Another animalistic base note was a glandular secretion originally sourced from a civet cat. When combined with other ingredients in minute quantities, this foul-smelling substance gave a perfume a new character and a surprisingly pleasing aroma. As with all scents derived from animals, civet is now a synthetically-reproduced aroma chemical widely used in contemporary perfumery.

Ambergris or 'grey amber' is a grey, waxy substance produced by the digestive system of the sperm whale. A sweet, earthy marine-like scent with a strong faecal odour, it was expelled by dead or sick whales and found floating in the sea, or washed ashore. It was used as a fixative and base note in perfumery.

Another animal ingredient, castoreum, was historically obtained from the dried castor sacs that the beaver uses to secrete a substance for marking its scent. It was used for its leather-like animalistic scent.

The first perfumiers and aromatherapists were priests, followed by physicians and medics. In early history, therefore, there was not always much distinction between perfume and medicine and they were used for both purposes. Over time, however, as trade routes increased and ingredients from around the world were more easily obtained, perfumes developed and became more sophisticated and perfume 'shops' were opened.

Queen Elizabeth I of England was particularly fond of perfumes and, as was the fashion with the ladies of the era, enjoyed creating her own fragrances. She was often seen wearing fashionable perfumed gloves and carrying a pomander scented with rosewater, benzoin, ambergris, civet, musk and other aromatic materials to prevent infection. During her reign, perfumes were also burned in rooms and used to fragrance sheets, while scented bellows were puffed around the room to scent the air.

During the eighteenth century, heavier perfumes gave way to lighter ones such as the famous Kölnisch Wasser (eau de Cologne), an Italian recipe manufactured in Köln, Germany, which changed the fashion of scents (see page 61 to recreate the recipe). It was loved by Napoleon who spent vast sums on expensive scents.

The perfume industry as we know it today was revolutionized in a small town called Grasse in the southern region of France. The 'capital of Provence' was originally an area for leather tanning, producing perfumed leather gloves which were the height of fashion in the seventeenth century. The fashion for the gloves declined with the introduction of leather taxes and, with the dawning of the Industrial Revolution, the perfume industry in Grasse developed rapidly.

In the nineteenth century perfume companies purchased vast areas of fields and turned them over to growing flowers such as jasmine, lavender, rose and tuberose, all hand-picked by locals at certain times of the day. More perfume companies moved to the edge of town, which attracted other associated businesses such as manufacturers of glass bottles and corks, and Grasse became the market leader in the supply of quality raw materials.

Advances in chemistry from the late nineteenth century onwards enabled perfumiers to create new scents using aroma chemicals, which replicate the more expensive and hard-to-find ingredients such as animal scents, rose or violet. Essential oils and absolutes were therefore used in smaller quantities and were added to provide richness and sophistication to a perfume.

The advent of the exciting new aroma chemicals gave perfumiers a much wider palette from which to create designer scents that were unique, complex and exciting. Perfumes were therefore cheaper to produce and more affordable for the masses. In the twentieth century this took the perfume industry to a new level and created the multi-billion pound industry it is today.

The sense of smell

During evolution, the human sense of smell (olfaction) has been somewhat lost. Unlike other animals, we no longer need to negotiate our environment by our sense of smell, or smell the scent of our enemy. We have fewer receptor cells than mice, but more than fish. Next time you see your dog's nose twitching, note that his olfactory epithelium is around 40 times larger than yours, which makes his sense of smell up to several million times more powerful.

Evolution has given all living organisms the essential survival tools or enzymes that bind to certain smells (odour molecules) to trigger a reaction or emotion. Odours can alert us to danger such as a fire or chemical spillage, or food that has gone off and may poison or kill us. Young mammals need their olfactory sense to detect their mother's milk for feeding. Some scientists now believe that the process of selecting a partner or mate may unknowingly involve the sense of smell via aromatic chemicals called pheromones.

When we breathe in odorous molecules they travel up the nose and past olfactory receptor cells sending electrical signals to the brain by nerve processes. This can instantly trigger distinctive memories and associations from the past, a childhood trip, a relative, a place of worship, home, or other memories both pleasant and unpleasant. Humans have somewhere in the region of a thousand different kinds of olfactory receptors, and can remember up to ten thousand different odours.

What is perfume?

The word perfume (parfum) derives from the Latin *per* meaning through and *fumum* meaning smoke, an indication of how early perfumes were produced by burning materials such as wood, gums and resins to give a fragrant smoke (incense), which is still used in places of worship and for meditation today.

A perfume is a blend of fragrant essences and oils obtained from flowers, grasses, resin, bark, gum, fruit, animals and aroma chemicals, dissolved in an alcohol or oil base. Different amounts of these oils are mixed with varying grades of alcohol and water to produce certain strengths such as toilet water, eau de Cologne, eau de toilette and the strongest and most expensive, eau de parfum and perfume. Perfumes, (fragrances) are also used to scent cleaning products, candles, pot pourri, talc, creams, soaps, cosmetics and bath products.

Commercial perfumiers choose from thousands of natural essential oils and synthetic aroma chemicals that are sourced from all corners of the globe. Used like the colours of an artist's palette, many ingredients may be selected and combined in their formulations and complicated blends to produce olfactory masterpieces. The process of perfume blending is highly skilful and complicated, taking years of experience and training and requiring a particular 'nose' for the job. Just one drop of a precious ingredient added, and left to blend for several days with its counterparts, may make the difference between an ordinary and an outstanding perfume.

Perfume classifications

A good starting point for creating your perfume is to decide its general category. The following classifications may help you to decide. Remember, however, that fragrances may contain aspects of different classifications.

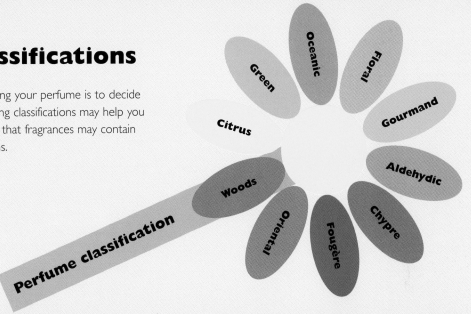

Floral	Geranium, jasmine, neroli, rose, ylang ylang, lavender
Oceanic	A modern classification with clean, crisp, ozonic aromas
Green	Light and fresh, with ingredients such as galbanum, estragon, violet leaf and helional
Citrus	Bergamot, lemon, lime, mandarin, orange and petitgrain
Woods	Woody scents such as sandalwood, cedar and patchouli
Oriental	Vanilla, florals and woody with animal scents, camphoraceous oils and resins
Fougère (meaning fern)	Oakmoss, lavender, coumarin, herbaceous and woody. Mainly men's fragrances
Chypre (meaning cypress)	Warm and woody with herbaceous, citrus, floral and animalistic notes. Oakmoss, amber, ambergris, civet, patchouli, bergamot and rose
Aldehydic	A family of aroma chemicals known as aldehydes
Gourmand	A modern classification of scents resembling food flavours with edible qualities. Notes of vanilla, chocolate and tonka bean

Creating your own blends

Blending essential oils to create your own fragrance to use in the following soap recipes does not have to be a complicated process. It is possible to create a unique fragrance blend from just a few ingredients.

Please note that the following instructions are to enable you to create your own scent for use in soaps. They are not perfumes or fragrances for spraying on the body. As with all essential oils, they should never be used neat on the body or in the bath.

The perfume industry uses mostly aroma chemicals in its complex formulas, and essential oils are only used in small quantities to enhance the perfume. This means that most perfumes or fragrance oils have little or no therapeutic effect. The instructions that follow will show you how to create your own essential oil blends which, using the practice of aromatherapy, may have therapeutic benefits.

You will not, however, be able to create your own fragrance oil using essential oils. If you would like to use a specific aroma, you will need a ready-made fragrance oil which has been produced with aroma chemicals. In this way, you will be able to scent your soaps with such delights as chocolate, apple, passion fruit, blueberry muffin, pina colada, mango or sea breeze (see the list of suppliers at the back of the book).

It is possible to mix fragrance oils together to create different scents. For example, a ready-made cinnamon and orange fragrance oil could be blended with a ready-made strawberry fragrance oil to create a 'mulled wine' fragrance. Several fruity fragrances could be used to create a 'fruit salad' fragrance. These fragrance oils will not have any therapeutic benefits: they are purely for fun and aroma pleasure.

Get to know your scents

First, become familiar with your essential oils and make sure that you keep notes of your findings. If you create a stunning fragrance, you will want to remember exactly how it was formulated.

When sampling an essential oil, do not place your nose directly over the top of the oil and sniff vigorously. If you do, the full blast of the molecules will go up your nose; the scent will remain in the nostrils for some time and it will be very difficult for you to test any more odours for a considerable period.

If you do test the scent directly from the bottle, it is also important to realize that this will not give you the full aroma, as you may only smell the top notes. To appreciate a fragrance fully, it is best to use paper testing strips, which are very easy to make. Aromas can smell quite different once they are out of the bottle, and sampling from a paper strip will allow you to sample the full aroma

Prepare some strips of paper (coffee filter bags are perfect) with which to absorb some of the oil. Waft the scented paper gently to and fro under your nose, allowing the fragrance to lift upwards, and breathe in slowly. You will usually only be able to sample around six scents at a time before you get nose fatigue. It is important to take regular breaks as essential oils are highly concentrated and sampling them for long periods at a time may cause headaches or nausea.

If your nose becomes overpowered, go outside in the fresh air to clear your nasal passages, or wave your hand over your nose to bring clear air into your nostrils. Remember that if you have a cold, or are a smoker, it will impair your sense of smell.

The notes in the previous essential oil section (see pages 42–51) will help you to describe the scents of your essential oil, but make a habit of writing down descriptions of the aromas that you experience. Blind testing yourself is always a useful and fun way of learning to recognise the scents of the different oils.

Top, middle and base notes

The fragrant ingredients used to create perfumes are categorised by their 'notes', like a beautiful piece of music for your senses. A fragrance, or perfume, is made up of top, middle and base notes.

The top or 'head' notes are small molecules and are the first that you notice when sampling a fragrance. Assertive, bright and initially strong, they stimulate the senses and are important in creating the first impression of a fragrance.

These volatile fresh, sharp top notes are powerful and intense to begin with, but are the first notes to disappear.

When the top notes begin to disappear, the middle notes start to come through. These generally warm, soft and mellow oils provide the heart and body of the fragrance, rounding it off and giving it complexity. They pave the way for the emergence of the next level of oils which taken in isolation can be quite unpleasant but, in partnership with the middle notes give support and durability.

The base notes, or 'theme', of the fragrance are usually heavy, exotic, intensely sensual and warm and are generally woody or resinous materials. These strong aromas are the last scents to be detected; they linger longest and 'fix' the whole blend, preventing the top and middle notes from evaporating too quickly.

Top		Middle		Base
bergamot	lemon	black pepper	lemongrass	cedarwood
bog myrtle	lemongrass	cardamom	marjoram	frankincense
cardamom	lime	chamomile roman	manuka	jasmine
clary sage	mandarin	clary sage	neroli	myrrh
cypress	manuka	elemi	palmrosa	patchouli
eucalyptus	neroli	fennel	petitgrain	sandalwood
fennel	orange (sweet)	geranium	pine	vetiver
geranium	petitgrain	ginger	rosemary	
ginger	peppermint	hyssop	rose geranium	
grapefruit	pine	jasmine	tea tree	
hyssop	rosemary	juniper	thyme	
juniper	rose geranium	lavender	ylang ylang	
lavender	yarrow			

Blending your perfume

First, decide on a theme for your therapeutic blend. Do not expect to be able to create the next famous fragrance the first time you blend essential oils; that would be a little like picking up a pen and paper and expecting to write Beethoven's 5th Symphony. Perfumery is far more difficult than it may appear, and it takes years of training and experimentation to create the perfect scent. With practice, however, you will begin to understand essential oils and how to blend them. If you persevere, you will be able to create your own unique scent.

To begin with, it is best to keep things simple. Try not to over-complicate your blend or create a cure-all recipe by using a multitude of oils and herbs. Focus on one aspect at a time: if you are suffering from stress, make a relaxing blend using a few essential oils that specifically target that complaint. Don't try to make something that will also ease your hangover, athlete's foot and PMT at the same time. Of course, if you are lucky, your therapeutic blend may help all these things!

Think about what gives you the most pleasure. If it is the scent of a flower, a walk through an orange grove, or a visit to a herb garden, use this to inspire your theme. There are so many ideas to choose, and the following recipes should help to point you in the right direction.

Once you have chosen your theme, use the essential oils directory (see pages 42–51) as a guide. Select your oils, beginning with the base oils, then the middle and finally the top notes – though some people prefer to start from the top and work down. Formulate your personal blend using scents that are relevant to your theme and which complement each other. The simple formulation charts on pages 60–61 should show you how to develop your perfume drop by drop.

Create your own unique scent for your soaps.

This means that if you are unhappy with the end result, it will be easy to replicate the stages of your blend and omit or replace the ingredients that you did not like. Write down each ingredient and the quantity you think you will use in a notebook.

On page 57 you will find a chart in which some common essential oils have been categorized into top, middle and base notes. Remember that this is only a guide, as oils vary from batch to batch depending on how they have been extracted, where they come from, and the species of plant. Some will therefore some will cross over the 'note' boundaries.

Find a good balance of top, middle and base notes. For example, do not overpower a precious jasmine with too many pungent spicy balsamic notes; let the 'celebrity' or special oils speak for themselves, and surround them with oils that support and enhance them. This takes practice and skill and also depends on personal preference.

There are, however, no hard and fast rules. Just one essential oil could be used alone, or two oils blended together. Remember that you are creating a scent for your personal pleasure. If you think your chosen oils blend beautifully together, then your fragrance is a roaring success, as you are the customer.

For your first formula, you may wish to take just three oils – a top, middle and a base note – see how they blend together, then add other ingredients, or change the amount of drops used for a second formula. Begin with simple blends, using only small amounts of oil so that you do not make expensive mistakes. When your confidence grows, you can use more oils in your blends.

Blending, using a bottle with a built-in dropper cap.

Using a bottle with a built-in dropper, or a pipette, drop the first essential oil you want to use into a clean bottle. Make sure the drop does not hit the sides of the glass bottle as it will cling to the sides for some time and you will not get the true quantity of oil in the bottom of your bottle.

You will need a different built-in dropper or pipette for each essential oil. If you dip the same pipette into different oils they will become contaminated and may ruin your precious essential oils. You can purchase replacement caps for essential oil bottles that have built-in droppers; these are perfect for this purpose.

To sample, dip a testing strip into your blend to soak up some of the fragrance.

Make sure that all your drops are the same size – a drop from a pipette held sideways will create a much larger drop than one dropped from holding the pipette straight above the bottle.

Approximate measures:
1ml = 20 drops
1tsp (5ml) = 100 drops
1 fluid oz (5 tsp) (25ml)

Blend suggestions

Feel Good blend

The following formula is a recipe used for 'La Vie en Rose' on page 113 which requires 2 teaspoons of the final blend, or very approximately 200 drops. Before adding the fragrance to the recipe, measure out the quantity you need carefully using your teaspoon measure. You will not necessarily need to use the whole amount that you have made.

If you decide that you want less of a base note, either decrease the patchouli, or add more rose geranium or palmarosa. Start the formula again, noting the revised number of drops in the second formula column.

Once you have developed your new fragrance, leave it for a few days if possible as the oils will react and blend with each other over this time.

FEEL GOOD BLEND			
Essential Oil	1st formula	2nd formula	3rd formula
Ylang ylang	12 drops		
Patchouli	30 drops		
Black pepper	10 drops		
Palmarosa	100 drops		
Rose geranium	100 drops		
Neroli	10 drops		
Total	262 drops		

Help Me – rescue blend

This blend is used for 'Cleopatra's Secret' on page 124. It uses oils that have been known since ancient times for their healing and preservative properties.

HELP ME – RESCUE BLEND			
Essential Oil	1st formula	2nd formula	3rd formula
Frankincense	40 drops		
Myrrh	20 drops		
Lavender	100 drops		
Elemi	20 drops		
Total	180 drops		

'Eau de Cologne' blend

There are many variations of this old-fashioned refreshing blend and in the table (right) are some of the traditional ingredients used in eau de Cologne. Try tweaking, adding or removing some of the oils on the right until you find a recipe that works for you. For inspiration, remember that the perfume was designed to have the odour of an Italian spring morning after the rain. You may also like to add a few drops of rosemary or clove essential oil.

EAU DE COLOGNE BLEND			
Essential Oil	**1st formula**	**2nd formula**	**3rd formula**
Bergamot	32 drops		
Petitgrain	30 drops		
Lemon	30 drops		
Neroli	10 drops		
Lavender	10 drops		
Orange	2 drops		
Total	114 drops		

Important note

Do not forget to label and date your blend and keep well away from children and pets. Store in a cool, dark place in a coloured glass bottle.

After several days, dip your testing strip into your blend and sample the fragrance, waving it gently under your nostrils. Leave the testing strip for a few hours, come back and sample again. If you are happy with the fragrance, use your new blend to create your own bespoke soap.

Herbs, botanicals and additives

For thousands of years civilisations have used the plants that surround them to heal, purify, beautify, prevent disease, and in religious ceremonies. In Egypt, China, Greece, Rome, India and Arabia plant essences, herbs, botanicals, resins and aromatic oils were used medicinally, for worship, in cosmetics and in perfumes.

Herbs from flowers, fruits, leaves, stems and roots have been used in herbal medicine practices including Chinese, Ayurvedic, Siddha and Tibb Unani. Such is the belief in the power of the plant, they are still practised and highly valued today. Other therapies that use nature's ingredients, flowers, herbs, oils and gums, such as aromatherapy, herbalism, flower remedies and homeopathy, are beginning to play an important part in healthcare alongside modern medicine. It is important to note however that these are 'complementary' therapies and should not be used in place of conventional medical advice and treatment.

Ancient art and manuscripts show that herbs were used in important religious ceremonies and banquets, in incense and sacrifice, and to anoint brave travellers on their journeys. The Romans valued them so highly that they took their favourites with them as they travelled, and plants that we still use today have been found in archaeological sites round the world. In ancient times aromatic herbal oils, resins and plant essences were more valuable than gold, and were often presented as gifts. The precious oils you owned, and anointed your body with, were evidence of your wealth.

Some people believe that locked within the plants that surround us is the ability to heal and cure, and with the destruction of many forests and the flora and fauna that grow beneath their canopies, these potential cures for illness and disease are disappearing. It is therefore wise to try and purchase not only the best ingredients, but those that are ethically and sustainably sourced.

Your own garden could be the source of many soap-making ingredients.

(Clockwise from top) dried, natural ingredients such as poppy seeds, pumice, charcoal and oats can all be used to add texture and colour to your soaps.

Customized soaps

You may have seen soaps for sale, but would rather have had a different colour, shape, texture or scent: now is your chance to create something exactly to your own specifications.

The following section will help you to choose herbs, botanicals and other additives so that the soap you make is exactly right for the person who is to use it. You may decide to take inspiration from one or two of the vast arrays of ingredients that are available from all corners of the globe.

You should also consider whether the soap is for a child, teenager, man or woman, sports enthusiast or couch potato, whether it is to help ease a particular ailment, or is simply a bar containing your favourite herbs and oils. Do not be tempted, however, to add every ingredient that relates to your ailment or theme: this will overload the soap and make it too complicated. Sometimes, a transparent soap with just one added herb or essential oil is, in its simplicity, just as pleasurable as one that is jam-packed with ingredients.

Common herbs, botanicals and other additives

Beeswax

Cera alba (refined white), Cera flava (yellow)

Beeswax is a natural wax that is secreted by young honey bees to produce the cells and walls of the honeycomb, and to cap cells in the hive that are full of honey. The colour varies from yellow to brown depending on the type of flowers visited by the bee and the location of the wax in the hive. Refined white beeswax is available from suppliers. Beeswax has been used throughout time for its anti-bacterial and antiseptic properties and to heal wounds. It will harden soap and has soothing, softening and emollient properties that help the skin to retain moisture.

Borage

Borago officinalis

Borage is commonly known as 'Starflower' because of its attractive blue star-shaped flowers, which are often used in summer cocktails. A hairy-leafed plant with a cucumber scent originating in the Mediterranean, borage was said to have been given to Roman soldiers and Crusaders for courage. It is known as an aphrodisiac and helpful for depression. Borage oil, which is made by infusing the leaves in a carrier oil, has been identified as one of the richest sources of Gamma-Linolenic Acid (GLA) which helps to repair the body. The oil is known to help inflammation, the hormonal system, pre-mentrual tension (PMT) and menopause. The dried herb may also be added to soaps for a rustic herbal look.

Burdock

Arctium lappa

Burdock belongs to the thistle group, and both the leaf and root of the plant are used. The seed pods, with their natural 'hook and loop fasteners' which attaches the seed to animals, are reputed to have been the inspiration for the invention of the modern-day nylon fasteners. Burdock is well used as a blood purifier and to minimise boils, acne, eczema, ulcers, scaly and inflamed skin.

Chamomile powder or flowers

Anthemis nobilis

Chamomile is a strongly aromatic white flower with a yellow centre, like a daisy, and an old favourite amongst garden herbs. The flowers are a pretty additive to the top of herbal or garden-themed soaps. The whole of the small flower is yellow when dried, and powdered chamomile will give soaps a flecked muted yellow colour. Historically, chamomile has been used for its sedative and relaxing properties and is known to soothe sensitive and irritated skin.

Cinnamon

Cinnamomum zeylanicum

Cinnamon powder is a reddish-brown powder obtained from the bark of a small evergreen tree native to the Indian subcontinent. It is used to fight exhaustion and depression and is a known to help alleviate the aching muscles that come with colds and flu. Cinnamon is said to stimulate the circulation and to benefit the aches and pains from rheumatism, arthritis and period cramps. However, use this spice sparingly – cinnamon is warming and stimulating but can irritate the skin if too much is used. It will give a rustic brown flecked colour to soaps.

Borage

Beeswax

Cosmetic clays

Mineral-rich clays have been used for centuries for their therapeutic and healing properties, leaving the skin clean, soft and detoxified. They are believed to help improve circulation, remove toxins and impurities, tighten pores and promote healing. Their powerful absorption properties makes them beneficial to those with oily skin, acne, spots or problem skin. Each type of clay has its own unique properties and contains different quantities of minerals and colour depending on the source. Not only are clays known to be beneficial to the skin, but they are also a good way of adding earthy colour and texture to your soaps. The following are the most common clays available for cosmetic use:

Bentonite clay

Bentonite, also known as montmorillonite, is a type of clay formed from naturally occurring volcanic ash sediments and contains more than 70 trace minerals. This is one of the most effective and powerful healing clays, and the largest and most active deposits come from Wyoming and Montana in the US.

Fuller's earth
Solum fullonum

Fuller's earth is a naturally occurring sedimentary clay with a high magnesium oxide content, often containing the mineral montmorillonite (see above). As with other clays, it draws out oil and toxins from the skin, so is a great additive to facial products for those prone to oily skin or acne.

Caution: Use only clays that have been purchased from a cosmetic or soap making supplier and not from art colour suppliers.

Kaolin (china clay)

Also known as white cosmetic clay or china clay, this is a fine and gentle mineral clay with natural absorbency properties. It is high in calcium, silica, zinc and magnesium, which are beneficial for oily, blemished skin. Kaolin has been historically used to reduce swelling, inflammation and to rejuvenate the skin giving it a healthy glow.

Montmorillonite (French clay)

Montmorillonite is the name of a mineral found in large quantities in bentonite clay (see left), but it is also the name of a classification of mineral clays formed from volcanic ash. These clays are typically made up of microscopic moisture-absorbing crystals that can swell to several times their original volume. Also known as French clay, it gets its name from Montmorillon in France and may be green, pink, yellow or white. The powerful moisture-absorbing properties are particularly good for oily or greasy skin, for drawing out impurities and toxins, and for toning the skin.

Rhassoul clay

Rhassoul is an ancient clay from the Atlas Mountains of Morocco with a long history of use in beauty care. It is a mineral rich, reddish/brown clay high in silica, magnesium, iron, calcium, potassium and sodium. With its wonderful power of absorption this clay is most beneficial for cleansing, toning and detoxifying the skin, making it a great addition to facial soap bars.

Montmorillonite clay: green and pink.

Cocoa (chocolate) powder

Theobrama cacao

This dark brown powder, also known as chocolate powder, comprises the non-fat components of the cacao bean which are known as cocoa solids. It is a high source of natural antioxidants, that are known to protect and nourish the skin. It has a deliciously sweet chocolate smell and gives a pale to dark brown colour to soap base – surely a must for all chocolate lovers. This is a great additive when combined with moisturising cocoa butter, the fatty part of the cacao bean that is separated from the solids at the beginning of the extraction process.

Comfrey

Symphytum officinale

Comfrey is a hairy-leafed plant, related to borage and forget-me-not, with light purple, cream or pink flowers. Both the leaf and the roots are used in herbal medicine and it is widely used as an organic fertilizer. It is famously known as 'knitbone' for its healing ability, and contains allantoin, a natural compound that promotes cell healing, the growth of healthy tissue and soothes, protects and softens the skin. Comfrey also contains mucilage – a gooey polymer that acts as a membrane thickener, – which is also found in aloe vera, cactus and marshmallow. This forms a soothing film over the mucous membrane, thereby relieving pain and inflammation. It is widely used in modern herbalism for healing broken bones, sprains, cuts, wounds, skin irritation and bruises, and to ease pain, inflammation, haemorrhoids and gout.

Comfrey

Dead Sea mud (Sediment)

Maris limus

The Dead Sea is a salt lake that lies between Israel and Jordan that was once part of the ocean. Its shores are the lowest natural point on earth. The salinity of the water is so high that fish and plant life are unable to live in it, hence its name. However, the water and the clay that make up its bed are rich in magnesium, potassium, calcium chlorides and high concentrations of bromides.

For thousands of years kings and queens have travelled far and wide to bathe in the Dead Sea. Its waters and mud are believed to be beneficial for the treatment of psoriasis, eczema, muscular pain, arthritis and rheumatism. If you want to create your own mineral-rich spa bars, Dead Sea mud can be added to your soap base to bring its benefits to your own bathroom.

Dandelion

Taraxacum officinale

The name is said to be derived from the French *dent de lion* meaning 'lion's tooth' due to the jagged, tooth-like leaves of the plant. In France the leaves are widely used in salads and the herb is named Piss-en-lit or 'wet the bed' which refers to its diuretic properties. Both the leaf and the root can be used. It has been used historically as a liver and kidney tonic.

Dried flowers

Most flowers and petals turn brown in soap and are therefore not usually used in the soap base. However, flowers can be used for decorative purposes by pushing or pressing the dried flowers or buds into the top of semi-set soaps. Among dried flowers that you might like to try are blue mallow or malva flowers, dried lavender, marigolds (*calendula*) jasmine flowers, rose petals or rosebuds

Flower Remedies

Bach Flower Remedies were developed in the 1930s by Dr Edward Bach, a Harley Street physician who was dissatisfied with orthodox medicine and inspired by homeopathy. He believed that certain plants infused in spring water and left in the sun to impart their properties, transmitted their 'energies' to the user. The flower-based remedies he created are intended to treat 38 negative states of mind. More recently, naturopath Ian White used his understanding of Australia's natural bush plants to create Australian Bush Remedies. These are said to dissolve subconscious negative beliefs, and restore balance to the mind, body and spirit.

Ginger powder
Zingiber officinale

Ginger is widely used in Chinese medicine, and is known to be stimulating and warming. It is known to be an anti-oxidant with aphrodisiac properties. Dried ginger is said to help colds, stomach pain, nausea, digestion, cough, rheumatism, arthritis, muscle ache and inflammation.

Ginkgo biloba
Ginkgo biloba

These large trees with bright yellow leaves have been cultivated in China for more than 1,500 years. Known as 'Silver Fruit', they are thought to improve memory and concentration, circulation, energy levels. They also act as a powerful antioxidant and anti-inflammatory.

Ginseng
Panax ginseng

Ginseng originates in Asia and means 'the wonder of the world' or 'all-heal'. It has been used in Chinese herbalism for thousands of years. Its wide range of uses include focusing the mind, fatigue, the immune system, stress, circulation and inflammation, as an aphrodisiac and a general healthy tonic for conditioning and rejuvenating the skin.

Grapefruit seed extract (GSE)
Citrus grandis

Not to be confused with grape seed extract, grapefruit seed extract is a thick dark liquid which is naturally derived from the seeds and pulp of the grapefruit. It is widely used to inhibit the growth of bacteria, mold and fungi as well as other organisms. It was developed by German-born researcher Dr Jacob Harich in 1963, as a natural way of preventing mold from growing on fruits and vegetables. The liquid form of GSE is also used topically for a variety of skin conditions including acne. Add ¼ teaspoon to each 1 litre or kilo (1¾ pints or 2¼ lbs) melted soap base.

Gingko biloba

Green tea

Camellia sinensis

Green tea has long been used in China, Japan, India and Thailand for digestion, lowering blood sugar and for healing wounds. It is known to be a powerful antioxidant and contains a wide variety of vitamins and minerals that help to protect the skin. It is also known to have skin rejuvenating and healing properties, and has been used to help athlete's foot, bedsores and skin disease.

Goat's milk powder

Caprae lac

Goat's milk is a natural emollient that helps to moisturize, nourish and soothe the skin. It is rich in vitamins A, B12, D and K and contains iodine, potassium, magnesium and selenium. Goat's milk is said to be extremely effective in soothing skin conditions such as eczema, psoriasis and dry skin, and is a wonderful additive to soaps.

Honey

Mel

Honey is a food source produced by the honey bee, obtained from the nectar of different flora and fauna in the environments surrounding the beehive. It is a mixture of sugars and other compounds, vitamins and minerals. The exact composition of each honey will vary according to the different mix of flower nectars obtained. It is best to warm honey slightly before adding to soap to ensure even distribution. From the earliest times, man has used the nourishing properties of honey to protect and heal. The sacred amber liquid has also been used in religious ceremonies and rituals. It has been used topically to heal for thousands of years and has proven antiseptic and anti-bacterial properties. In fact, it is even now used in hospitals for wound care, to help to combat MRSA and other bacterial infections. Some studies suggest that it may also help in the treatment of burns by helping to reduce healing time and scarring. Others claim that eating local honey may help to relieve the symptoms of hay fever.

Hops

Humulus lupulus

A well-known native British plant, hops are used as an additive in the beer-making process. Hops are known to possess sedative properties and are valuable in aiding sleep and as a traditional cure for insomnia. They also help to ease nervous complaints, relax muscles, improve the appetite and soften the skin.

Green tea powder

Goat's milk powder

Kelp powder

Laminaria digitata

Kelp are large nutrient-rich sea plants (algae), commonly referred to as seaweed. Abundant in amino acids, iodine and vitamins, kelp is used to tone, detoxify, moisturize, revitalize the skin and boost immunity. This powdered marine plant will leave browny-green flecks of seaweed throughout your soap, so it is a great additive for spa or ocean-themed bars. It will generally smell strongly of seaweed, however, so make allowances for this when fragrancing your product. Do not add too much to your soap as it will produce an odorous bar.

Lemon peel powder

Citrus medica limonum

Lemon peel powder can give a good natural colour to your soaps and can enhance any citrus oils used to fragrance your recipe. Rich in Vitamin C, lemon is used in alternative medicine to help the immune system, colds, infection and influenza, to detoxify, assist lymphatic drainage, digestion and as a skin tonic.

Kelp powder

Lemon balm

Melissa officinalis

Lemon balm has heart shaped, deliciously lemon-scented leaves that can be used as a substitute for lemons in cooking. Lemon balm was an ingredient in Carmelite water or 'Eau de Carmes', a perfumed toilet water created by Carmelite Monks in the seventeenth century, which was also taken internally for nervous headaches and neuralgia. It is known to be effective for the nervous system, depression, memory, headache, insomnia, herpes, colds and fevers, and insect bites.

Linden

Tilia vulgaris

Known as the lime tree, the linden grows to a height of up to 40 metres (130 feet) and should not be confused with the tropical lime fruit trees. The tree produces fragrant flowers which have been used for centuries to treat nervous conditions, anxiety, nervous headaches, insomnia, high blood pressure and stress. It is also used to ease colds and fevers, and to treat dry skin.

Loofah

Luffa

Loofahs look like sponges, but are in fact the dried interior tissues of gourd-like vegetables that are grown on the vine in Africa and Asia. You can embed a whole piece of loofah or add shredded loofah to your soaps. This will create a rough texture to exfoliate dead skin cells and increase circulation leaving the skin smooth and soft.

Shredded loofah

Marigold (Calendula)

Calendula officinalis

Calendula are the only flower petals that retain their colour in soap and are an attractive additive to either clear or white soap bases. The sunny orange-yellow petals of the marigold are a traditional remedy for minor skin problems such as cuts wounds and grazes and as well as providing beneficial skin-conditioning properties, Calendula has long been used to help inflamed skin such as acne and sunburn and as a herbal remedy for athlete's foot, thrush and fungal conditions. It has also been used historically to help prevent infection from spreading and to speed up the process of cell regeneration.

Milk thistle

Silybum marianum

Milk thistle is rich in essential fatty acids and is a powerful antioxidant. It contains silymarin which is known to decrease inflammation and to help to combat free radicals. It is best known for its ability to heal the liver. As it is believed that certain skin conditions may be the result of liver malfunction, milk thistle is often recommended for topical use to aid liver problems.

Dried marigold petals

Nettle

Urtica dioica

This herbaceous flowering plant has stinging hairs that give it the name 'stinging nettle'. The leaves are high in nutrients such as vitamins A, C and D, iron, potassium, manganese, calcium and nitrogen and once cooked, or crushed, the chemicals in the leaves that cause the sting are destroyed. Like mallow and comfrey, nettle contains the emollient polymer mucilage, plus minerals, formic acid, beta carotene and phosphates. Nettle has a long history and a multitude of uses. Roman soldiers carried the seeds of the plant with them when they travelled as it was so useful to them. It is recorded that they rubbed nettle leaves on their skin to treat cold, aching limbs. In the past, nettle fibres were used to make sails, sacks and linen and to produce a permanent green dye.

Nettle is used as an astringent and a stimulating tonic particularly for the hair. As a diuretic it is said to stimulate the kidneys and bladder and detoxify the body. It is known to help the symptoms of gout and arthritis and to stimulate the immune system. It is used either in dried leaf form for texture or powdered form for a natural green colour in your soaps.

Dried nettle leaves

Oats

Avena sativa

Oats are the seed of a cereal grain, the extract of which is used in many topical skincare applications for eczema and psoriasis. Historically, it has been used to help to manage dry and itchy skin conditions. Adding rolled oats to your soap base can create a wonderful texture and can also offer gentle exfoliation, leaving the skin soft and silky. Rolled oats can be ground to a finer texture using a food processor if desired.

Pumice

Pumice

Pumice is a solidified frothy volcanic rock that is produced during volcanic eruptions. In its powdered form, it is a useful natural abrasive and exfoliant when added to soaps. It is particularly good for use in foot and hand scrubs for the removal of hard, dry skin.

Rooibos (Red bush) tea

Aspalathus linearis

This caffeine-free red herbal tea is unique to the Cedarberg mountains in South Africa. The reddish-brown needle-like leaves are high in antioxidants, and have been used historically in South Africa to relieve eczema, skin disorders and inflammation and to boost the immune system. Added to soap, rooibos provides an attractive fleck, texture and natural colour.

Wheatgrass powder

Triticum vulgare

This vivid green powder is obtained from the dried young sprouting leaves of wheatgrass. It is packed full of vitamins, minerals and enzymes and contains a high proportion of chlorophyll, hence the colour. It is known to be beneficial for the immune system, and is reported to remove toxins from the body, help acne and scars, and restore damaged skin tissue.

Whey powder

Powdered whey is a cream-coloured fine powder which is made by dehydrating the liquid left after straining curdled milk. Rich in valuable amino acids, minerals, vitamins and lactic acid which regulates the pH of the skin, it is known to be effective for smoothing dry scaly skin, for stimulating and deep cleansing the skin cells and for soothing eczema, psoriasis and sunburn. Cleopatra was famous for her beautiful skin which was reputedly obtained by frequently bathing in a luxurious milky bath.

Wheatgrass powder

Whey powder

Basic ingredients

Colour

You can, of course, leave your clear or white soap base uncoloured. White represents cleanliness, peace and purity and contains a little of every colour in the visible light spectrum. Without our conscious awareness, however, colour can play an important role in our lives, affecting our moods and sense of well-being. The Ancient Egyptians and the Chinese are said to have used colour for healing 'cures', though the idea was lost for a long time. Recently, however, people have again become aware of the importance of colour in our lives, and colour therapy plays an important part in businesses, hospitals, prisons, and the design of product ranges.

Some colours can relax and calm, while others can stimulate and revive. Visualizing colour can also affect the sense of smell. Try an experiment: make a batch of uncoloured soaps fragranced with sweet orange. Colour half with orange and leave the other half white or clear. Ask your friends and family to try and guess which has the strongest smell, and you will probably find that the majority of people will perceive the coloured soap to have the strongest scent.

It is widely known that colour can also influence mood. A vase of vibrant red flowers in the middle of a dining table will promote lively conversation, energy and a successful dinner party. Pale blue flowers will promote a calm, relaxing atmosphere.

Once you have chosen the theme and scent of your soap you can finally choose the colour. Choose a colour that will naturally complement and enhance your soap, for instance a gardener's hand scrub would make sense if coloured green, and seaweed spa bar would be enhanced by shades of blue or turquoise.

Colour associations

Different colours are believed to be associated with various parts of the body, helping to ease problems in certain areas. It is said that you are often drawn subconsciously to a particular colour that relates to a problem that you are experiencing.

Red: power, passion, love, excitement, circulation, adrenalin, reviving, energy. Known to help muscle aches, lethargy and tiredness.

Blue: calming, restful, peace, relaxation. Known to help the throat, upper arms and lungs.

Orange: gentle strength, optimism, creativity, promotes change. Known to help the lower back, kidneys, abdomen, bronchitis.

Turquoise: Affairs of the heart, panic, shock, restorative. Known to help areas of the throat and chest.

Yellow: alertness, depression, laughter, joy, fun, cheerful, revitalising. Known to help the stomach, liver, digestive system, detoxification, depression.

Purple: protection and leadership, spiritual awareness, concentration, rejuvenation. Known to help the head, scalp and immune system.

Green: harmonizing, shock, fatigue, healing, balance, stamina. Known to help the heart, chest and lungs.

Pink: the colour pink contains red and will have the same properties of red but with a more gentle effect, such as love, warmth, nurture and tranquility.

Basic ingredients

Colouring soaps

There are various ways to colour your soaps. Remember that the base colour may be affected by essential oils, fragrance and additives, so always add the colour at the last stage. If desired you can then add liquid cosmetic colour, coloured pigments, micas, natural herbs or spices, or clays.

Liquid colours

The easiest cosmetic colours for use in soaps are liquid cosmetic colours. For the recipes in this book you will need cosmetic grade liquid blue, red, yellow and green. Some liquid colours may bleed into the next colour or into the soap base, and non-bleeding colours are also available from soap suppliers. These colours can be blended together to create different shades (see the colour mixing chart on the facing page). If you have nothing else available, you can use liquid food colouring from your kitchen cupboard, but these are not always reliable and may fade quite quickly. For the best results, cosmetic grade colours are recommended.

Cosmetic liquid colours can be blended to create your own shade. A selection of liquid colours available from soap-making suppliers.

Simply add liquid colour drop by drop, until you achieve the required colour. Stir the soap thoroughly to make sure that all the colour has been mixed in OR stir only slightly to achieve a marbled effect.

Clays and powdered herbs

These are a great way to introduce natural earthy colour to your soap while at the same time adding therapeutic benefits. Mix the powdered ingredient with a little water before adding to the soap base to prevent the powder clumping.

Annatto powder will add a yellow colour to your soaps.

Natural colours derived from plants

Powdered forms of plants, herbs and spices can be used to add colour and texture to soaps. The list of natural ingredients is almost endless. Some ingredients may react with the soap base, fragrance or oils and affect the overall colour of your soap, and you may need to experiment a little to achieve the desired colour. The recommended quantity to add to the basic recipe (see page 24) is up to one tablespoon of powdered herbs per kilo or litre (1¾ pints or 2¼lbs).

Alkanet (Alcanna tinctoria) root, a plant in the borage family, produces a pink/purple colour in soap.

Colour mixing chart

You will need to make allowances for the actual colour of your essential oil, fragrance and additives such as herbs or oils. For example, many of the base notes are very dark brown, some of the citrus oils are yellow or orange, and roman chamomile and yarrow essential oils are blue. Bear this in mind when using colour as different additions may change the colour of the finished soaps.

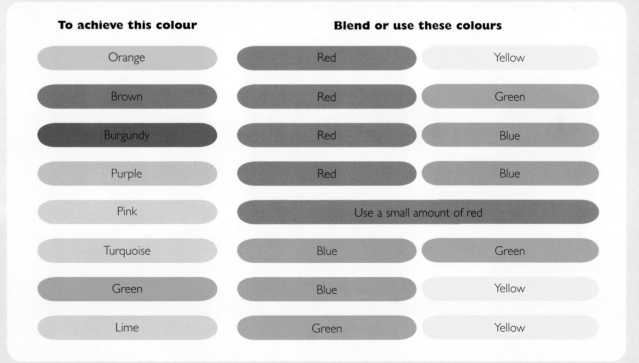

To achieve this colour	Blend or use these colours	
Orange	Red	Yellow
Brown	Red	Green
Burgundy	Red	Blue
Purple	Red	Blue
Pink	Use a small amount of red	
Turquoise	Blue	Green
Green	Blue	Yellow
Lime	Green	Yellow

Pigments

Pigments are powdered colours made up of small particles. These are the ultramarines, the oxides and the chromium greens. These powdered substances were originally mined from earth and rocks and contained high levels of toxic and unsafe minerals. These days, they are synthesised for use in the cosmetics industry so that they are chemically identical to the pure substance but are safe and non-toxic. Pigments are strong and dense and do not generally fade as fast as liquid colours; a tiny amount goes a very long way. As they are made up of fairly large particles they are not suitable for clear soaps, but may be used for opaque soaps with a rustic look. Mix with a little water before adding to soap base to prevent clumping.

Pigments, from top, clockwise: Ultramarine Pink. Chromium Green Oxide, Utramarine Violet and Ultramarine Blue.

Titanium Dioxide

Ultramarines
Ultramarine Light Blue
Ultramarine Pink
Ultramarine Violet

You may also see ultramarine blue rather than light blue for sale. This is best avoided as in certain recipe combinations using regular blue can smell like bad eggs. Choose light blue or 'odour-free'.

Oxides
Iron Oxide

Chromium Green Oxide (green chrome oxide)

Hydrated Chromium Oxide (Hydrated Green Chrome Oxide) – a green/blue

Black Iron Oxide

Yellow Oxide

Titanium Dioxide (white)

Note: white soap bases differ from clear bases only in the addition of Titanium Dioxide to make the soap white. It is therefore a useful stock ingredient. To make a white soap base, blend titanium dioxide very well with water and stir into the soap base thoroughly: if the soap is too hot or has not been blended well enough some particles can sink to the bottom.

Cosmetic glitters and micas

There are many different-coloured cosmetic glitters available which can add colour and sparkle to your soaps. Only cosmetic grade glitters should be used: hobby craft glitters are not suitable for bath products. Large shaped glitters such as hearts or stars are not recommended for adding to soaps as they may have sharp edges that could scratch the skin. To add glitter, just sprinkle them into your soap base and stir. Some large-particle glitters may sink a little: to prevent this, keep stirring the soap until it cools and thickens a little before pouring, or use a 'suspending' soap base.

Mixing mica with water.

Cosmetic glitters (top) and micas (bottom).

Mica powders are very fine particles which can add a beautiful pearlescence or iridescence. They are available in many colours and can also add a pale colour to your soap. Mix with a little water before adding to the soap base to prevent clumping. Micas and glitters can be used together to add sheen, lustre and sparkle to your soaps. Micas and glitters can be used in both clear and opaque soaps, but will generally create the most stunning effects in clear soaps.

Caution

- If you are using glitters in soaps remember that they should be kept away from the eyes.

- Colours and their strength may vary from supplier to supplier, so use a colour sparingly the first time until you get used to its intensity and behaviour.

- Remember that natural ingredients are just that: natural ingredients. Some can fade quite quickly. Do not leave soaps or ingredients in direct sunlight as it may destroy fragrance and colour.

- The 'raw' colours are strong and intense and only a little is needed. It is wise to cover clothing and work surfaces when handling colour and wash any areas of contact straight away to avoid staining.

Vegetable oils and butters

Nature has provided an abundance of gifts for healing and protecting our skin in the oils and butters contained in the seeds, nuts and kernels of plants from all over the world. These include African shea butter, Asian mango butter, Chinese rice bran oil, macadamia nut oil from the US and olive oil from the Mediterranean.

Throughout history, as revealed in ancient Egyptian, Roman and Greek literature, oils extracted from plants (known as vegetable oils), have played an important part. These oils and butters contain valuable nutrients, and are still used today to nourish, moisturize, soothe, pamper and revitalize dry and sensitive skin.

The skin is responsible for eliminating waste, and products containing or derived from petroleum can block the pores and make it difficult for toxins to escape. Natural vegetable oils work with the body's chemistry, and many are high in antioxidants which are believed to help to combat the destructive effect on the skin of free radicals caused by pollution, cigarette smoke and the sun's ultra-violet rays. Others are known for their therapeutic and skin-renewal benefits and are used to treat skin conditions such as eczema and psoriasis, aching muscles, or to help the appearance of scars and wrinkles.

Vegetable oils

Vegetable oils are traditionally obtained by pressing, crushing and often refining the seeds, nuts and kernels of plants and are liquid at room temperature. These essential parts of the plant's system contain high levels of different fatty acids, vitamins and minerals and have known antioxidant, anti-inflammatory and moisturizing properties.

The traditional and natural cold pressing method of oil extraction yields the best quality oil from seeds, leaving it as close as possible to its natural state. Oil is literally squeezed or pressed out of the seeds and then filtered to remove the sediment or seed husks, which are often used for animal feed. Oils produced in this way have more colour, flavour and odour and retain most of their nutrients. Olive oil can be produced by this method and on your supermarket shelf you will be able to see the difference in colour between a cold-pressed extra virgin (first pressing) olive oil and a regular olive oil.

Other more modern methods use high temperatures or petrochemicals such as hexane, a hydrocarbon with potential carcinogenic properties, to extract the oil. This method requires high refining which results in the removal of many of the nutrients such as essential fatty acids, chlorophyll and vitamins. Traces of petrochemicals may also be retained in the oils.

The versatility of vegetable oils is legendary and they have a multitude of uses. Apart from their obvious use in the in the food industry, many oils are widely used to make soaps, skin care, cosmetics and candles. Vegetable oils have also been used historically to make paint and to treat wood and are now widely used as lubricants, electrical insulators and in the production of biodiesel.

On the next few pages are some of the most popular and luxurious oils and butters that you might like to add to provide that extra element of decadence and pampering to your soap.

Vegetable butters

A 'butter' is a naturally sourced hard vegetable fat obtained from the kernels, or nuts, of plants which is solid at room temperature. The term is slightly misleading as it has nothing to do with dairy products normally associated with the word butter. High in healthy essential fatty acids, vitamins and minerals, butters are a luxurious ingredient in the cosmetics and body care industries. To use butters in your soaps, they should be heated gently until they are liquid. Instructions on how to melt your oils are on given on page 26, Step 6.

Most vegetable glycerine soap bases will be made from a combination of vegetable oils, usually coconut and palm oils, and the addition of a little extra precious oil or butter can be added either for their therapeutic properties or to nourish, moisturize, soften and protect your skin. However, care should be taken not to add too much extra oil to your soap base as your soap may become too soft and the lather may be reduced due to the heaviness of the excess oils. We would recommend adding approximately a maximum of 1 tablespoon of liquid oil or butter to a litre or kilo (1¾ pints or 2¼ lbs) of melted soap base.

Note: Do not expect oils or butters to smell of the original fruit or plant, such as mango or raspberry, as the familiar scent is not usually retained in the refined butter. Each will, however, have a unique aroma. Make allowances for this when scenting your soaps, as it could affect their fragrance.

Cocoa butter

Directory of common oils and butters

Apricot kernel oil

Prunus armeniaca

This light, pale oil is pressed from the kernel of the apricot fruit. It is readily absorbed into the skin and is similar to sweet almond or peach oil. High in essential fatty acids, linoleic and oleic acids, it is said to be beneficial and nourishing to sensitive, dehydrated and mature skin. It is used in skin-care for treating fine lines, delicate and sensitive areas.

Argan oil

Argania spinosa

The nut kernels of ancient Argan tree, found in the dry desert conditions of Morocco and North Africa, are hand-pressed to produce this oil. Similar in properties to olive oil, argan oil contains fatty acids and high levels of Vitamin E, a powerful antioxidant. The oil has been used for centuries by the Berber people to nourish and protect the skin and to promote its elasticity, thereby helping to reduce the appearance of scars and wrinkles.

Avocado oil

Persea gratissima

Avocado oil is obtained by pressing the flesh of the fruit. It is easily absorbed into the skin and widely used for sun-damaged or dehydrated skin, eczema and psoriasis. Its emollient properties make it ideal for rejuvenating and softening mature skin.

Babassu oil

Orbignya oleifera

The fruit of a palm similar to the coconut palm that grows wild in South America. It is prized locally for its moisturizing properties and used to treat dry and inflamed skin. A non-greasy emollient, it coats the skin leaving it silky and smooth and is also effective for oily skin.

Carrot tissue oil

Daucus carota

This golden yellow/orange oil is extracted from the flesh of the carrot. Rich in vitamins and beta carotene, it is a powerful antioxidant known to be extremely useful for cell regeneration and for those with dry, cracked and ageing skin. This strongly coloured oil can also be used to add colour to your soaps.

Castor oil

Ricinus communis

Obtained from the castor bean, castor oil acts as a humecant, drawing moisture to the skin and providing a protective barrier against the environment. Castor oil is also used for sunburn, skin irritation, burns and cuts and is reputed to ease various ailments such as inflammation and muscle pains.

Avocado oil

Castor plant

Cocoa butter

Theobroma cacao

Cocoa butter is the fatty component of chocolate, which is produced from the cacao bean. The name *Theobroma* means 'food of the gods' and anyone who is a chocoholic will understand why.

Cocoa solids (chocolate powder) and cocoa butter are separated at the early stages of production for use in different manufacturing processes. They are also brought together again and used in the production of chocolate. Cocoa butter on its own is used to make white chocolate.

Unrefined cocoa butter has a dark creamy colour and a fantastic chocolaty aroma – you will have to use all your willpower not to eat it! The most widely available is the white, refined, cocoa butter that has no smell. This is useful if you want most of the nutrients cocoa butter provides but do not wish your products to have a chocolate smell. Cocoa butter is said to provide a protective barrier to retain the moisture in your skin. As a source of natural antioxidants it is known to help dry skin and wrinkles. It's also often used in sun tan lotions, and in skin-care to help stretch marks and scars.

Evening primrose oil

Oenothera biennis

This pale yellow oil is produced from the seeds of the evening primrose flower. High in gamma-linolenic acid (GLA or omega-6) it is used to help ease eczema, psoriasis and dry skin. Evening primrose oil is easily absorbed by the skin and used in skin preparations to prevent premature ageing.

Flax seed (linseed) oil

Linum usitatissimum

This light brown oil is high in the natural antioxidants vitamin E and Omega 3, and has valuable skin strengthening and nutritional properties. It is known for its anti-inflammatory properties which can help minimize the appearance of scarring, stretch marks, redness, acne, eczema and psoriasis.

Grapeseed oil

Vitis vinifera

A by-product of the winemaking industry, grapeseed oil is made from the seeds of grapes. It is easily absorbed into the skin and used in the cosmetics industry to support cell membranes, reduce the appearance of stretch marks, and to help repair damaged skin tissue.

Basic ingredients

Evening primrose

Grapeseed oil

Hazelnut oil

Corylus americana

This oil is pressed from the nuts of the hazel, which is grown in Northern Europe and has long yellow catkins that appear in the spring. The vitamin-rich oil has excellent emollient properties and contains high levels of thiamine (vitamin B1) and vitamin B6. Hazelnut oil has long been used for the treatment of dry, damaged skin and is reportedly helpful in filtering the rays of the sun. It is used in many sun-care products.

Hempseed oil

Cannabis sativa

Hempseed oil is extracted from the seeds of the hemp plant which is high in important unsaturated fatty acids including palmitoleic, oleic, linoleic and GLA. It is widely used in cosmetics due to the unique balance of its essential fatty acids (EFAs), which complements the proportion of EFAs required by the human body. Hempseed oil is reported to help reduce inflammation and to ease the symptoms of eczema and psoriasis.

Jojoba oil

Simmondsia chinensis

Jojoba is a native shrub from the deserts of Arizona, California and Mexico. The oil is actually a liquid wax obtained from the seeds of the plant. Jojoba oil is similar to sebum, the protective oily substance secreted by sebaceous glands, so it is readily absorbed by the skin. It is often used in the cosmetics industry as a fragrance carrier oil and as a moisturizer in skincare products. Rich in proteins and minerals, jojoba is used to help soothe eczema, psoriasis, dry and sensitive skin.

Kukui nut oil

Aleurites moluccana

This oil is traditionally used in Hawaii to rejuvenate, moisturize and nourish dry, mature and damaged skin. Kukui nut oil contains vitamins A, C, and E and provides antioxidants that help to protect the skin. A non-greasy oil, it is said to ease sunburn, eczema, psoriasis and dry sensitive skin.

Macadamia nut oil

Macadamia ternifolia

This oil is produced from the nuts of a native American tree. It contains high levels of palmitoleic acid, a substance similar to sebum, the oily substance secreted by the sebaceous glands to combat dryness and protect the skin from the growth of microorganisms. Production of sebum reduces with age, resulting in drier skin. Macadamia nut oil is a known treatment for mature, dry and ageing skin, as well as stretch-marks and burns.

Hazelnuts

Jojoba oil

Mango butter

Mangifera indica

Grown mainly in Myanmar (Burma), Southern Asia and Northern India, mango butter is obtained from the fruit kernels of the tropical mango tree. It has many applications including the treatment of dry, sunburned skin, to aid protection from the sun, and for wounds, rough skin, scars, wrinkles, eczema, psoriasis and dermatitis.

Monoi de Tahiti

Cocos nucifera – Gardenia tahitensis

The French Polynesians produce Monoi de Tahiti oil by the process of 'enfleurage', using exotic petals from their native tiare flowers gently macerated in refined coconut oil. This ancient method produces an exquisite, sweet floral aroma so it is a delightfully fragrant and moisturizing additive for soaps. Many inferior copies of this oil have been sold, so Monoi de Tahiti is now a registered Appellation d'Origine and carries a logo assuring of its authenticity and quality.

Neem oil

Azadirachta indica

This brown oil that originates from India has a strong, pungent odour. Traditionally used to treat skin disorders such as eczema, psoriasis, rashes, burns and acne, it is known to be antiseptic, antifungal, antibacterial and antiviral. It is also used in shampoo to control dandruff and lice.

Olive oil

Olea europaea

Grown mainly in the Mediterranean, olive oil is a green to golden brown colour depending on the quality. It is a complex compound made of fatty acids and is high in oleic acid, vitamin A, vitamin E (a natural antioxidant), vitamin K and other important vitamins and minerals. Its properties are said to be helpful for burns, inflammation, arthritis, wounds, and dry skin.

Pomegranate seed oil

Punica granatum

The seeds of the pomegranate fruit are packed full of antioxidants that fight free radicals and skin ageing. The oil is used to moisturize and heal dry, mature cracked skin. It is said to help fight lines, wrinkles and sunburn and to aid regeneration of skin cells, helping to strengthen and nourish the epidermis and promote the skin's elasticity.

Mango butter

Monoi de Tahiti

Pumpkin seed oil
Cucurbita pepo

This oil is made by pressing the roasted, hulled pumpkin seeds and is usually a very dark green sometimes referred to as 'green gold'. It is an extremely nutritious and nourishing oil, and contains many important active constituents – high in essential fatty acids, omega-3, omega-6, zinc, and vitamins A, C, and E. Vitamin E is a powerful antioxidant that can help to diminish the appearance of stretchmarks and wrinkles and ease the effects of psoriasis.

Raspberry seed oil
Rubus idaeus

Extracted from the seeds of the raspberry fruit, raspberry seed oil is reputed to be an excellent antioxidant, high in essential fatty acids and vitamin E which is known to play an important role in the repair of skin damage. Its anti-inflammatory properties are superior to those of many other oils, and it is particularly useful in facial skincare, as an emollient and to help to soothe eczema, rashes and overheated, irritated skin. It also reputedly acts as a UV filter and is a valuable ingredient in sunblocks and sun-screens.

Rice bran oil
Oryza sativa

Extracted from the germ and inner husk of rice, rice bran oil is a mild and softening oil that has long been used in Japan to protect and moisturize mature or sensitive skin. It is high in essential fatty acids and vitamin E and offers excellent antioxidant properties. Rich in oleic and linoleic acid, it is known to help inflammation, dry and ageing skin.

Rosehip oil
Rosa canina or *Rosa moschata*

Obtained from the seeds of rosehips which contain high levels of vitamin E, this oil also contains essential fatty acids and retinol (vitamin A), which is said to help delay the effects of skin ageing. It is widely used in skincare products for its regenerating properties, and is known to help dry, damaged, scarred skin, pigmentation and stretchmarks.

Shea butter
Butyrospermum parkii

This rich, creamy natural fat is obtained from the fruit of the African Karite Tree. It is used to help diminish the appearance of skin blemishes including scars, stretchmarks, burns, rashes and eczema. A highly emollient butter rich in nutrients, it is prized for its anti-ageing and moisturizing properties.

Pumpkin seed oil

Rosehips *Shea butter*

Strawberry seed oil

Fragaria vesca (or Fragaria ananassa)

This luxurious oil contains some of the most powerful sources of antioxidants found in nature, is high in gamma tocopherol and is a valuable source of essential fatty acids such as linoleic, alpha-linoleic and oleic acid making it a wonderful anti-ageing ingredient. Highly emollient with a light texture and subtle aroma, this oil is effective for dry and damaged skin.

Sweet almond oil

Prunus dulcis

This oil is pressed from the kernels of the sweet almond plant and has been prized since ancient times. It is widely used as a carrier oil as it is non-greasy and easily absorbed by the skin. Sweet almond oil contains vitamins A, B1, B2 and B6 and E. It is a wonderful emollient used to nourish, protect and condition the skin, to calm skin irritation, and to soften dry skin.

Vitamin E oil

Tocopherol

Vitamin E is a fat-soluble antioxidant found in a variety of fruit and vegetables. It is known to protect against cell-damaging free radicals, which are caused by pollution, fried food, smoking, stress, sunbathing, infection and stress. It is claimed that vitamin E also helps to reduce the appearance of stretchmarks, age spots, scars, dry ageing skin and keeps the skin looking younger by reducing the appearance of lines and wrinkles.

Wheatgerm oil

Triticum vulgare germ

This emollient oil is expressed from the germ of the wheat kernel and is high in essential fatty acid, vitamins E, A, D, and linoleic acid (omega-6). The nourishing oil is known for its antioxidant properties which help to detoxify and protect the skin from environmental pollutants. It is used to condition dry, cracked skin and to repair sun-damaged, dehydrated and sensitive skin.

Almonds growing

Wheatgerm oil

Recipes

After hours of dancing the night away, look after those weary feet and keep your tootsies in tiptop condition by using one of these scrubby soaps to soothe and soften your feet and heels.

Well Heeled

See pages 24–35 for basic soap recipe instructions

Ingredients

1 litre or 1kg (35oz) melted white soap base
100g (3½oz) pumice powder
Red liquid colour
2 teaspoons lemon verbena essential oil
1 teaspoon petitgrain essential oil

Moulds

Shoe-shaped moulds (as used for making chocolates)
Alternative: margarine tub or food storage container

Additional instructions

Keep stirring the mixture until it cools slightly. The pumice powder is heavy and may sink slightly but the thicker (cooler) the soap, the less it will sink.

Make treasured gifts for loved ones by using moulds shaped like little gifts, or wrap plain rectangular soaps in cellophane and decorate them with beautiful ribbons and bows.

Present and Correct

See pages 24–35 for basic soap recipe instructions

Ingredients
1 litre or 1kg (35oz) melted white soap base
1 teaspoon gold mica (blended with a little water)
1 teaspoon cosmetic grade gold glitter
1 teaspoon olive oil
1 tablespoon (or 4 teaspoons) Festive Spice fragrance oil

Moulds
Present-shaped moulds (as used for making chocolates)
Alternative: any small square or rectangular plastic mould

Other ideas
Finish off a plain square mould by tying ribbon round the soap

These moisturizing hand soaps are made with silky shea butter, which helps dry skin, eczema and psoriasis. Pretty cosmetic glitter could be added for a 'designer handbag', as a special treat for a guest bedroom.

Pretty Handy

See pages 24–35 for basic soap recipe instructions

Ingredients

500ml or 500g (17½oz) melted white soap base
Liquid colour of your choice
1 teaspoon cosmetic-grade glitter (optional – see page 77)
1 teaspoon melted shea butter
2 teaspoons Champagne fragrance oil
   (or your favourite designer fragrance)

Moulds

Handbag or purse-shaped moulds
   (as used for making chocolates)
Alternative: yoghurt pots

Other ideas

Try adding several different coloured glitters to give a sequin rainbow effect.

Diamonds are a girl's best friend but, if you can't afford bling, why not make your own treasure? Be really creative, blending, swirling and layering different colours to resemble inclusions within the gems.

Precious Gems

See pages 24–35 for basic soap recipe instructions

Ingredients

300ml or 300g (10½oz) melted clear soap base

Any liquid gem-like colour (red, blue, green, orange, purple, yellow) or leave clear

1 teaspoon fresh, ozonic fragrance such as Rainforest or Summer Rain

Moulds

'Cool Jewels' ice cube tray with three-dimensional diamond shapes

Additional instructions

Use an ice cube tray or any small deep mould and cut the sides of the soap to look like the facets of gemstones.

Other ideas

Make holes in the soaps with a wooden skewer and thread ribbon through to create a soap necklace.

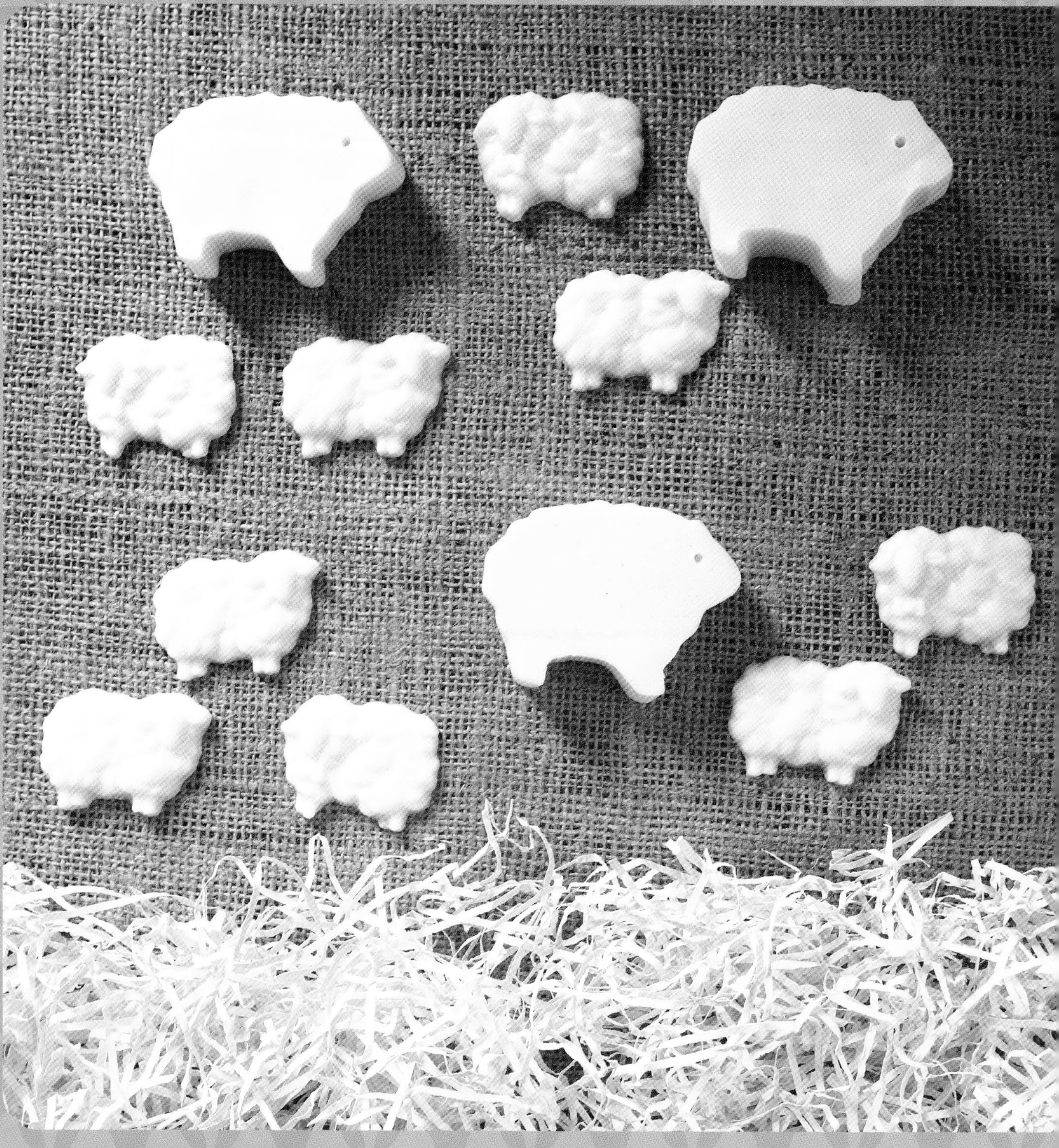

These soothing sheep should help promote a good night's rest and happy dreams. Place a few by the side of your bed and, if the calming scent doesn't send you to sleep, you can always count them!

Ewe and Me

See pages 24–35 for basic soap recipe instructions

Ingredients

1 litre or 1kg (35oz) melted white soap base
2 teaspoon organic lavender essential oil
½ teaspoon yarrow essential oil
3 tablespoons sheep's powder (or goat's milk powder)
   blended with a little water

Moulds

Mini sheep guest bar moulds
Sheep cookie cutter

Additional instructions

Pour the guest moulds first, then fill a plastic-lined tray with the remainder of the mixture and cut out the soaps using the cutter while still soft. Add a teaspoon of warm water to the melted soap to enable them to be cut out more easily.

Other ideas

Suitable alternative fragrances include mandarin or chamomile essential oil

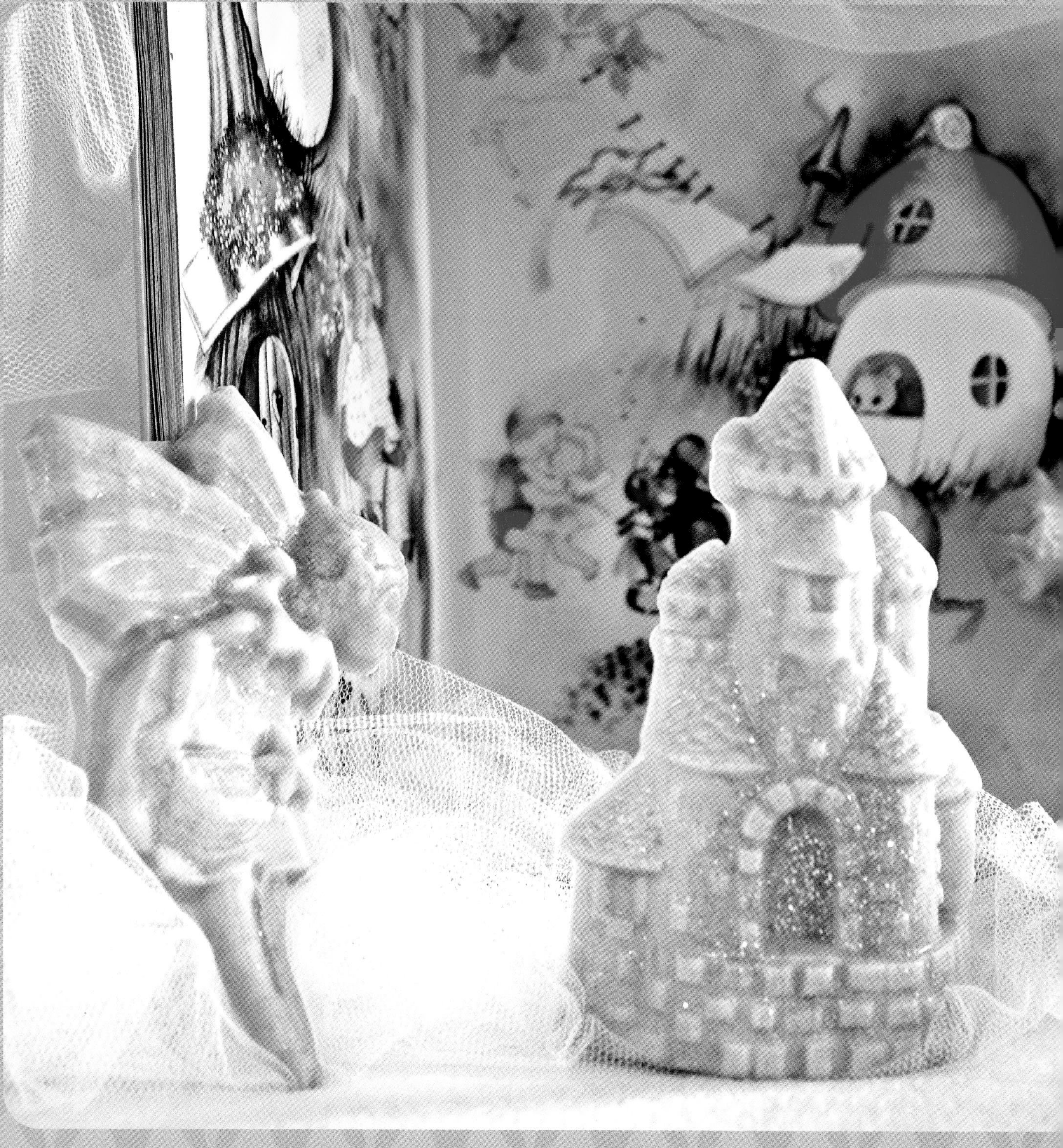

This shimmering, glittering fairy castle is every little girl's dream.
It probably contains a princess, a wicked witch, a few frogs, a prince,
a magic mirror and lots of spells – and a happy ending of course.

Fairytale

See pages 24–35 for basic soap recipe instructions

Ingredients

500ml or 500g (17½oz) melted white soap base
2 teaspoon Fairy Toadstools fragrance oil
1 teaspoon cosmetic grade glitter
1 teaspoon pearlescent mica (mixed with a little water)
Purple liquid colour

Moulds

Fairy castle (as used for making chocolates)
Fairy soap mould

Other ideas

Add the liquid colour, a few drops at a time, to achieve the desired colour. Add a teaspoon of water to the mixture and pour into a baking tray lined with plastic food wrap. When just set, cut out the soaps using fairy-shaped cookie cutters.

The knobbly bits on these clever soaps massage weary muscles if you have been running, skipping, hopping or jumping. The zesty citrus oils are invigorating, uplifting and deodorizing.

Good Sport

See pages 24–35 for basic soap recipe instructions

Ingredients

1 litre or 1kg (35oz) melted clear soap base
2 teaspoons may chang essential oil
2 teaspoons grapefruit essential oil

Moulds

Massage bar soap mould

Other ideas

Any of the citrus oils, including lemon, mandarin, lime, lemongrass, tangerine or clementine may be used.

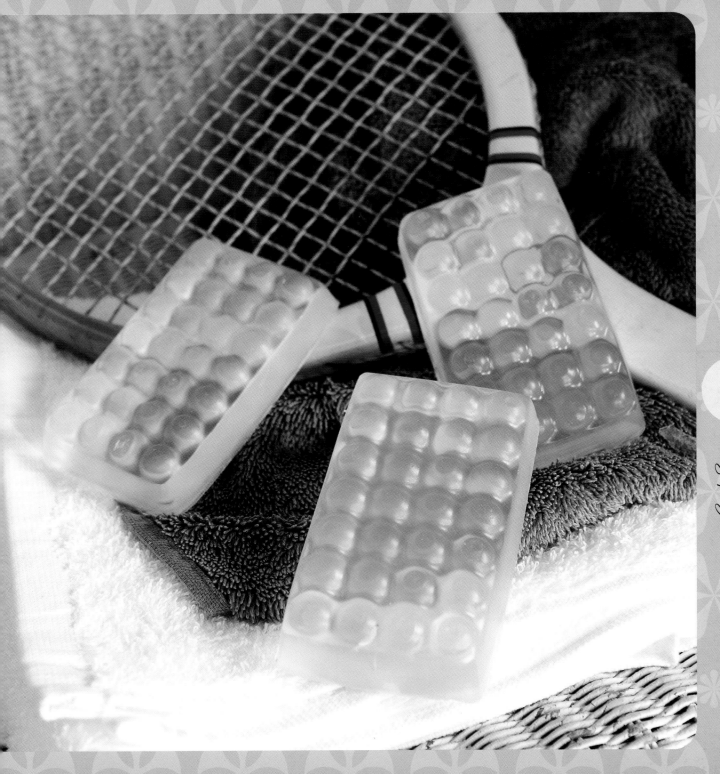

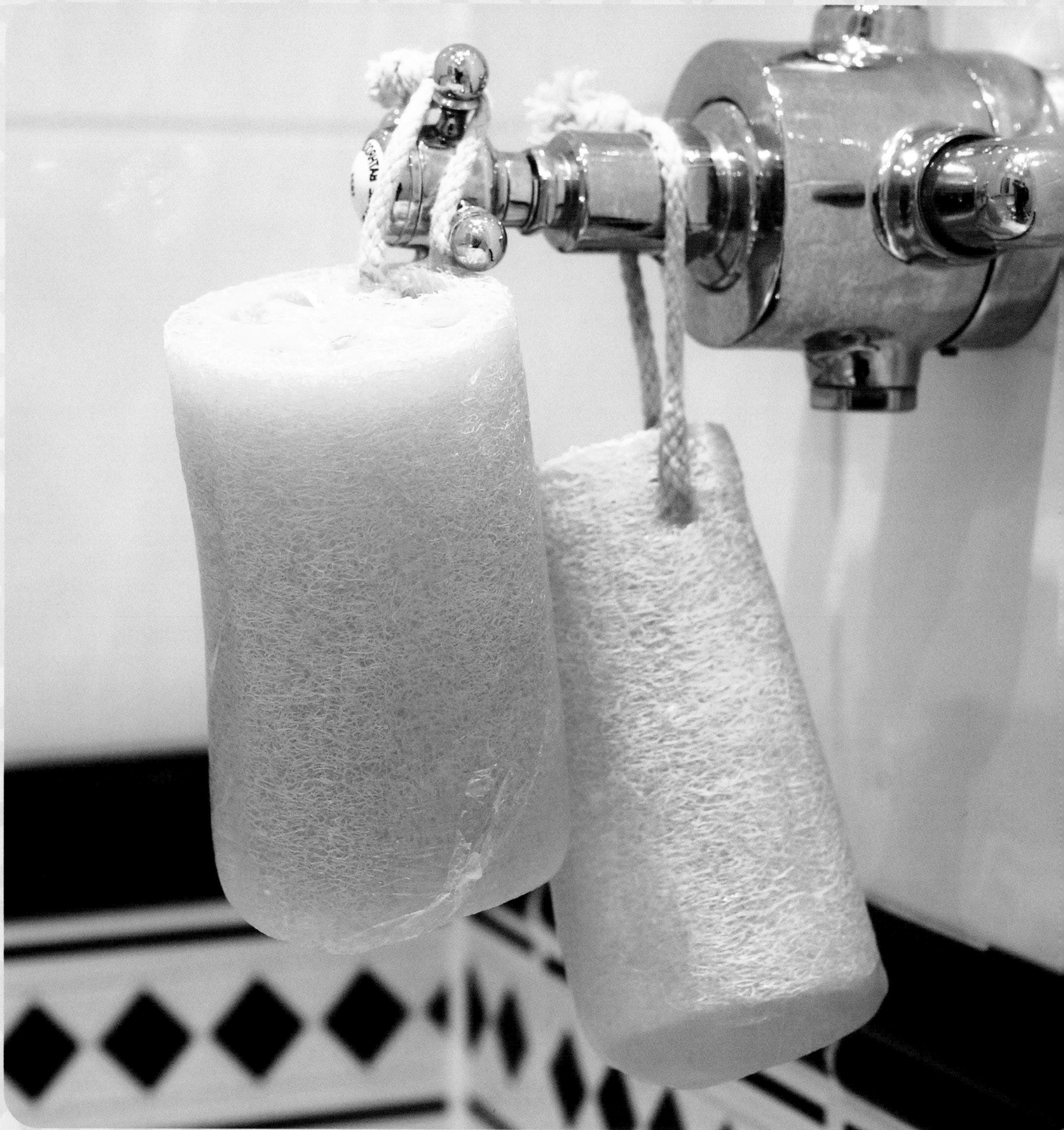

Vegetable loofahs make an ingenious base for a soap on a rope to hang in the shower. Great for exfoliating the skin and removing dead skin cells, they leave your body feeling silky smooth and healthy.

Feeling Ropey?

See pages 24–35 for basic soap recipe instructions

Ingredients
1 litre or 1kg (35oz) melted clear soap base
2 loofahs with rope loops (available from chemists
   or drug stores)
2 teaspoons lime essential oil
2 teaspoons lemongrass essential oil

Additional instructions
Wrap each loofah securely in plastic food wrap leaving the top part exposed. Place in a tray in case of leakage and pour the soap mixture in the top making sure that the rope is not sitting in any soap. Leave until thoroughly set, then remove the food wrap.

Other ideas
Use any other citrus oil such as lemon, mandarin, may chang, grapefruit, tangerine or clementine.

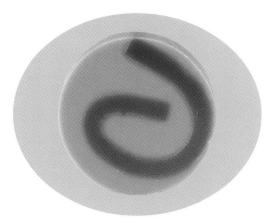

Coffee is said to be stimulating and full of antioxidants, so wake yourself and your skin before breakfast with a shot of caffeine in the shower. It's a great pick-me-up for tired skin after a late night.

Café Latte

See pages 24–35 for basic soap recipe instructions

Ingredients

500ml or 500g (17½oz) melted white soap base
2 tablespoons milk or whey powder blended
    with a little water
¼ teaspoon organic fair trade instant coffee
    (blended with a little water)
½ teaspoon black coffee fragrance oil
½ teaspoon chocolate truffle fragrance oil

For the swirl

300ml or 300g (10½oz) melted white soap base with
    1 teaspoon water added
1 teaspoon organic fair trade instant coffee
    (blended with a little water)
1 teaspoon of black coffee fragrance oil
1 teaspoon of chocolate truffle fragrance oil

Additional instructions

Make the swirl using the instructions on page 29. Spritz with surgical spirit and place inside a clean crisp/potato chip tube. Make the rest of the mixture and, when cooled, slightly pour into the mould around the swirl.

Get your chocolate fix without putting on a single ounce with these cute cup cakes. Full of antioxidants and skin-soothing properties, the only problem is that they are so pretty you won't want to use them.

Cup Cakes

See pages 24–35 for basic soap recipe instructions

Ingredients
For the soap cherries
A little clear soap
A few drops of red colouring

For the 'chocolate' soap base
250ml or 250g (9oz) melted white soap base
2 teaspoons organic fair trade cocoa powder
    (blended with a little water)
1 teaspoon vanilla extract essential oil
1 teaspoon melted cocoa butter

For the topping
250ml or 250g (9oz) melted white soap base
A few drops red liquid colour
1 teaspoon chocolate fudge fragrance oil

Moulds
Silicone fairy cake/muffin moulds or fairy cake soap moulds

Additional instructions
Soap cherries: colour a little clear soap red, pour into a container and leave to set for a few minutes. While still pliable, take small pieces and shape them into small rounds. Leave until required.
'Chocolate' soap base: make up, then pour into the bottom half of the moulds and leave to set for a few minutes.
Topping: tint the mixture pink with a few drops of red colouring. Pour onto the chocolate base and leave to set for 5 minutes. Spritz the cherries with surgical spirit and gently press onto the cakes.

> **CAUTION: Keep these soaps well away from young children who might decide they look good enough to eat.**

This recipe contains green tea, which has been used for centuries in the traditional Japanese tea ceremony. It is a wonderful antioxidant and contains many vitamins and minerals.

Tea Time

See pages 24–35 for basic soap recipe instructions

Ingredients

500ml or 500g (17½oz) melted white soap base
1 teaspoon Matcha powdered green tea
   (blended with a little water)
2 teaspoons green tea fragrance oil
1 teaspoon rice bran oil

Moulds

Teacup, saucer and teapot (as used for making chocolate)
Alternatives: cup from child's plastic teaset, lined with plastic
food wrap; empty margarine tub

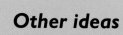

Other ideas

If you cannot find Matcha powdered green tea, cut open a teabag containing green tea and use the contents

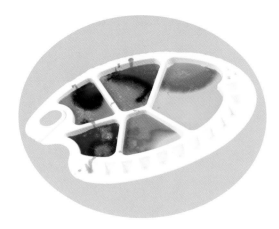

Let your imagination run riot and create stunning masterpieces fit for a gallery using an artist's palette as a mould. Swirl and marble rainbow colours together to create beautiful stained glass effects.

Fine Art

See pages 24–35 for basic soap recipe instructions

Ingredients

Mix 1
250ml or 250g (9oz) melted clear soap base
   (add 1 teaspoon of water to give more pouring time)
A few drops colour
1 teaspoon fragrance

Mix 2
250ml or 250g (9oz) melted clear soap base
   (add 1 teaspoon of water to give more pouring time)
A few drops of a contrasting colour
1 teaspoon fragrance

Additional instructions

Make up the two mixes in two separate plastic jugs. Pour the two colours into the moulds at the same time and swirl to create a marbled effect. Leave until just set, remove from the mould and, while still pliable, shape into your own shapes.

Moulds

Artist's plastic palette
Alternative: small plastic tray or margarine tubs.

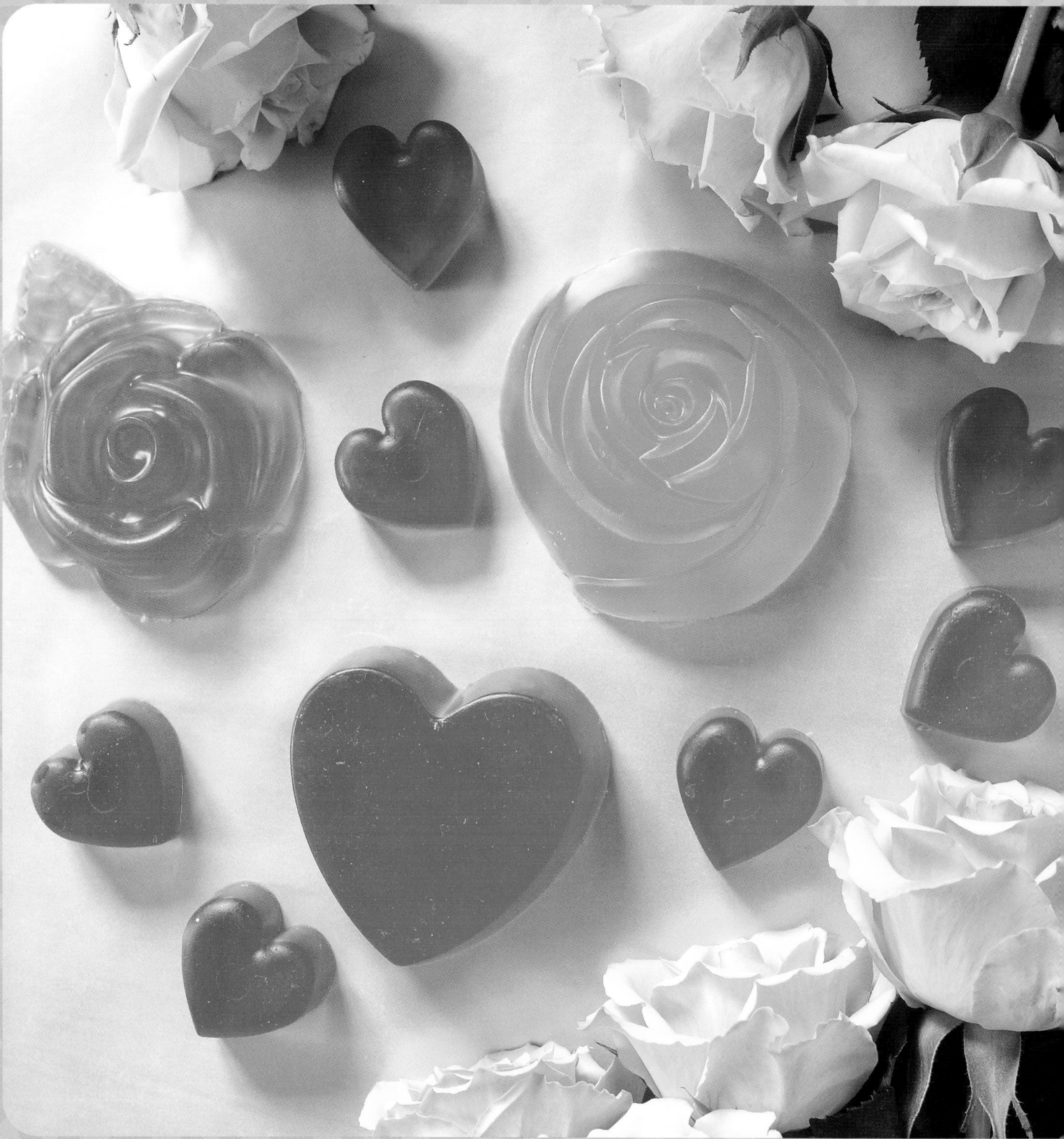

The rose is a symbol of love and beauty, and rosehips are used in skin care to promote cell renewal. This sensual and comforting blend of essential oils will lift and soothe spirits and moisturize dry, rough skin.

La Vie en Rose

See pages 24–35 for basic soap recipe instructions

Ingredients
500ml or 500g (17½oz) melted clear soap base
Red liquid colour
1 teaspoon rose hip oil
2 teaspoons 'feel-good' aromatherapy blend
  (see page 60 for recipe)
¼ teaspoon of Wild Rose Bach Flower Remedy

Moulds
Rose and heart-shaped soap moulds, heart ice cube moulds
Alternative: any plastic mould such as a yoghurt pot,
margarine tub or food container.

Additional instructions
Add the red colour carefully, a few drops at a time,
to achieve the desired effect.

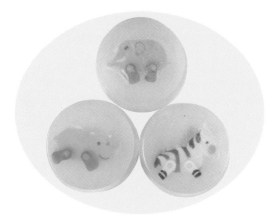

Let your imagination take a road trip with this safari-themed soap bar that makes great use of children's fun erasers. The same technique may also be used with other mini-soap embeds.

Safari

See pages 24–35 for basic soap recipe instructions

Ingredients
500ml or 500g (17½oz) melted clear soap base
Children's fun erasers or other small items
2 teaspoons clear fragrance oil or essential oil

Moulds
Any suitable mould

CAUTION: Make sure the melted soap is not too hot before pouring over any small objects that may melt.

Other ideas
Many small objects can be embedded successfully in soap, including coins, photographs, stamps, erasers, charms messages, tickets and other memorabilia

Mysterious and wonderful things from the bottom of the deep blue sea are a fascinating showpiece for your embedding skills – you have to make the sea creatures and shells before you can embed them.

Aquarium

See pages 24–35 for basic soap recipe instructions

Ingredients
Tiny soaps for embedding

For the sea bed
200ml or 200g (7oz) melted white soap base
1 tablespoon pumice powder
A few drops yellow colour
1 teaspoon Blue Lagoon fragrance oil

For the 'water'
300ml or 300g (10½oz) melted clear soap base
A few drops of liquid blue or turquoise colour
1 teaspoon Blue Lagoon fragrance oil.

Moulds
Any loaf mould, margarine tub or food container

Additional instructions
Make a selection of embeds in various shapes including starfish, shells and tropical fish.

Make and pour the sea bed layer and leave for a few minutes to set slightly. Spritz the layer and place some small embeds on top.

Make up the soap base for the water. Spritz the small embeds, then pour in the clear blue soap mix, placing more embeds carefully as you go. If the embeds will not stand up in the molten soap, leave to set for a few minutes and then push them in from the top.

CAUTION: Take care when pushing embeds into the hot soap base.

A trip to a relaxing spa is a perfect treat but, if you can't manage one, this recipe will cleanse your skin and clear your mind, and help you to create a mini spa in your own bathroom with the aroma of a luxury retreat.

Spa Bar

See pages 24–35 for basic soap recipe instructions

Ingredients

500ml or 500g (17½oz) melted white soap base
1 teaspoon rosemary essential oil
1 teaspoon organic English lavender essential oil
1 teaspoon sweet almond oil
1 teaspoon kelp powder (seaweed)
A few drops turquoise or blue liquid colour (optional)

Moulds

Margarine tub

Other ideas

Using essential oils of your choice, try creating your own therapeutic spa blend by following the instructions on how to blend on pages 58–59.

These little soaps are a great incentive for reluctant youngsters to wash, and also double up as a bath toy – let your little ones go quackers trying to fish the duck out of the tub.

Don't Forget to Duck!

See pages 24–35 for basic soap recipe instructions

Ingredients

For the duck

300ml or 300g (10½oz) melted clear or white soap base

A few drops yellow liquid colour

1 teaspoon English Rain fragrance oil

For the pond

300ml or 300g (10½oz) melted clear soap base

A few drops blue liquid colour

1 teaspoon English Rain fragrance oil

Moulds

Duck-shaped mould

Round soap mould

Additional instructions

Make up the ingredients for the duck and leave to set until hard. Make up the ingredients for the pond, pour into moulds and leave until a skin forms on top of the soap. Using a knife or skewer, make a hole in this skin.

Spritz the duck, then place gently on top and leave to set.

CAUTION: Can be used for age seven upwards. Use less, or no fragrance, for younger children.

Don't Forget to Duck!

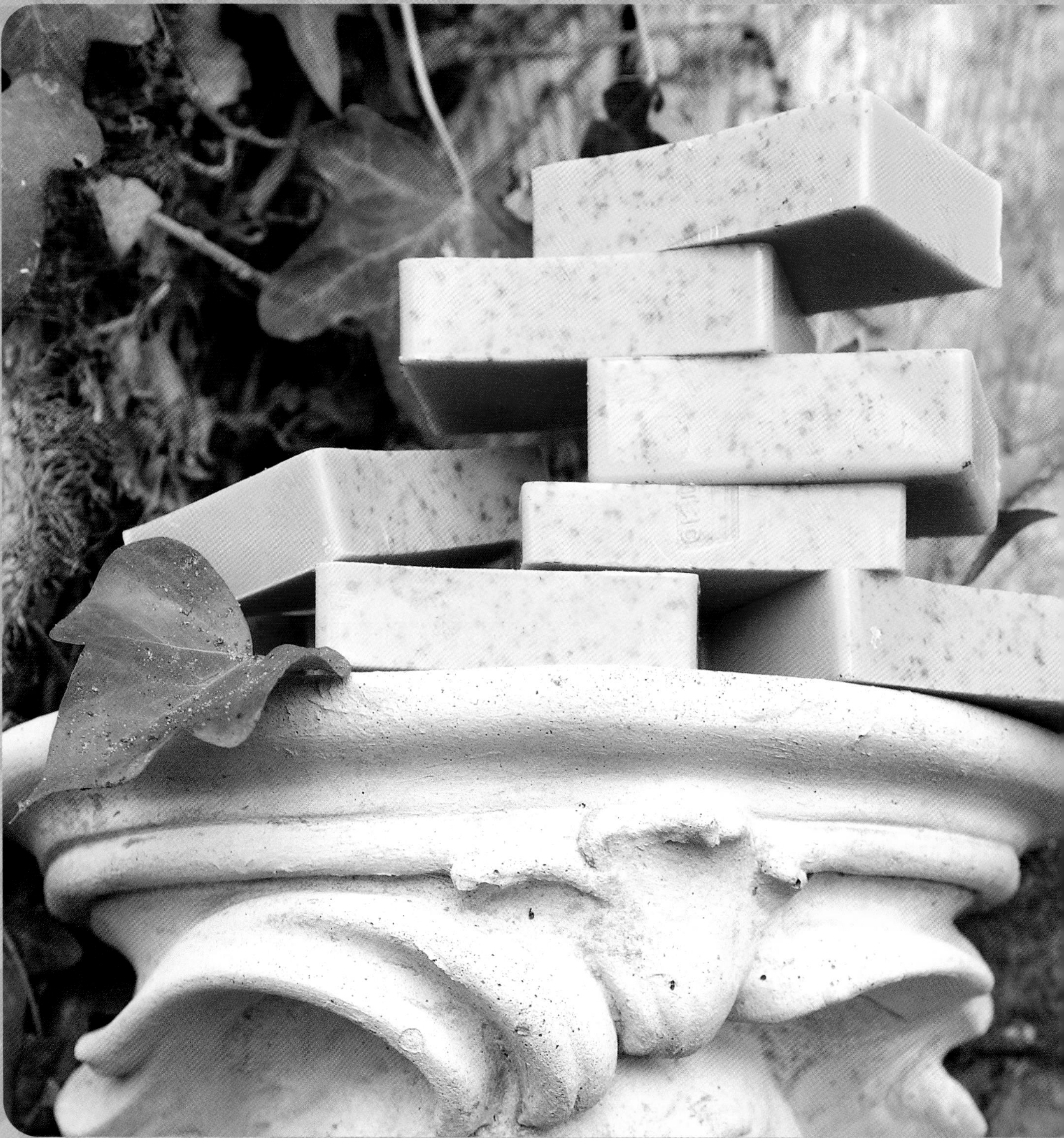

If you are in need of a little nurturing and pampering why not turn to the healing power of Mother Earth. Made with nature's ingredients, these comforting soaps will help to revive and restore.

Mother Earth

See pages 24–35 for basic soap recipe instructions

Ingredients

1 litre or 1kg (35oz) melted clear soap base
¼ teaspoon vitamin E
½ teaspoon evening primrose oil
1 teaspoon sandalwood essential oil
1 teaspoon frankincense essential oil
1 teaspoon lemon essential oil
¼ teaspoon manuka essential oil
1 teaspoon pink French clay (mixed with a little water)
A few drops red colour (optional)

Moulds

Plastic drawer tidy or margarine tub

Other ideas

Create your own own facial bar using some of the clays found in the herb section on page 65.

The Egyptians were known for their use of precious oils and perfumes. Indulge yourself with ingredients used since ancient times for their skin-enhancing properties.

Cleopatra's Secret

See pages 24–35 for basic soap recipe instructions

Ingredients

500ml or 500g (17½oz) melted clear soap base
2 teaspoons 'Help Me !' blend (see page 60).
1–2 teaspoons gold mica (blended with a little water)
1 teaspoon castor oil

Moulds

Pyramids and Egyptian-style mummies

Other ideas

This can also be made using white soap base if an opaque effect is preferred

Turn to the kitchen garden and use your favourite medicinal herbs and flowers to make a cleansing herbal hand scrub fit for the finest apothecary in town.

Herby Hand Scrub

See pages 24–35 for basic soap recipe instructions

Ingredients

500ml or 500g (17½oz) melted white soap base
1 teaspoon tea tree oil
½ teaspoon marjoram essential oil
½ teaspoon lemon grass essential oil
1 teaspoon hemp seed oil
1 teaspoon dried nettle leaf
4 tablespoons pumice powder
1 teaspoon green clay (blended with a little water)
1 teaspoon comfrey powder (blended with a little water)

Other ideas

If you do not have dried nettle leaf to hand, root through your cupboards and use any herbal tea bag such as chamomile or peppermint.

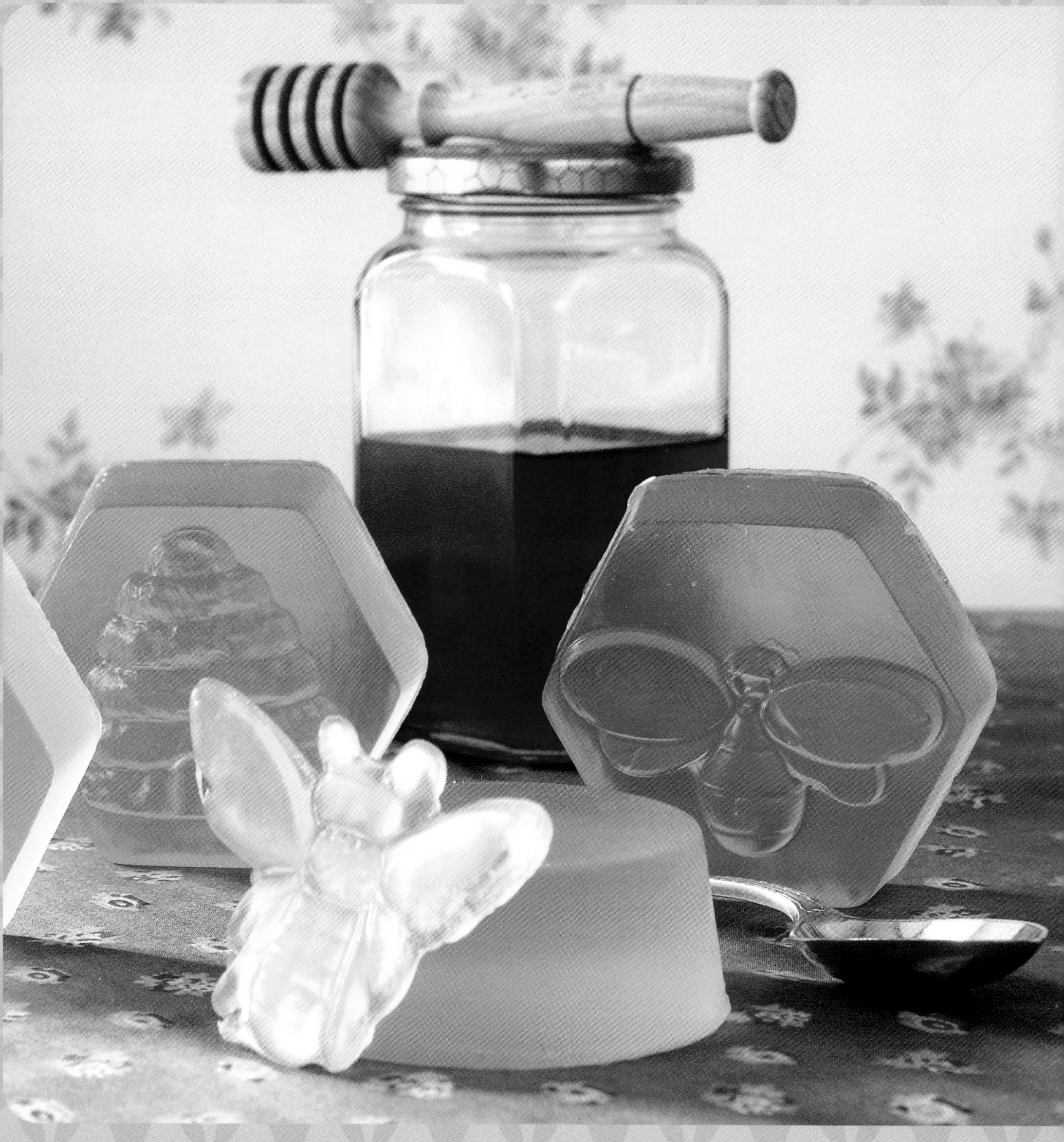

Honey has been used for centuries for healing wounds and to moisturize the skin. Create a buzz with these amber-coloured nectar bars which will help nourish and protect dry skin.

Bee Happy

See pages 24–35 for basic soap recipe instructions

Ingredients

400ml or 400g (14oz) clear melted soap base
2 tablespoons honey
3 drops orange liquid colour
3 drops yellow liquid colour
2 teaspoons amber fragrance oil

Moulds

Various bee-themed moulds
Alternative: any plastic mould

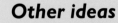

Other ideas

To make a harder bar, you could add some beeswax

Close your eyes and take an invigorating walk through an ancient
pine forest fragrant with the scent of spruce, bark and earth.
The aromatic oils will set you up for a day's work in the urban jungle.

Pine for Me

See pages 24–35 for basic soap recipe instructions

Ingredients

1 litre or 1kg (35oz) melted clear soap base
1½ teaspoons sandalwood essential oil
½ teaspoon cypress essential oil
½ teaspoon pine essential oil
A few drops liquid green colour

Moulds

Stackable pine-tree chocolate-making mould
Cookie cutters

If you have stars in your eyes look no further. This glittering soap with calming mandarin oil will let you float out to space and back again from the comfort of your own bathroom.

Shooting Star

See pages 24–35 for basic soap recipe instructions

Ingredients

For the soap stars
300ml or 300g (10½oz) melted white soap base
1 teaspoon clementine or mandarin essential oil
A few drops yellow liquid colour

For the swirls
250ml or 250g (9oz) melted white soap base
   (add 1 teaspoon water to give flexibility)
Few drops yellow liquid colour

For the glitter soap
1 litre or 1kg (35oz) melted clear soap base
4 teaspoons clementine or mandarin essential oil
1 teaspoon gold glitter

Moulds
Small star ice-cube moulds
Loaf tin or plastic drawer tidy
Plastic tray

Instructions
Make the soap stars and leave to set. Pour the swirl mix into a plastic tray and leave to set until just pliable. Cut into strips and curl around the handle of a spoon.

Make up the glitter soap base and pour a little in the bottom of a plastic-lined loaf tin or other mould. Spritz the stars and swirls and place a few in the bottom. Spritz again and pour in more glitter soap. Repeat, adding stars and swirls until the mould is full.

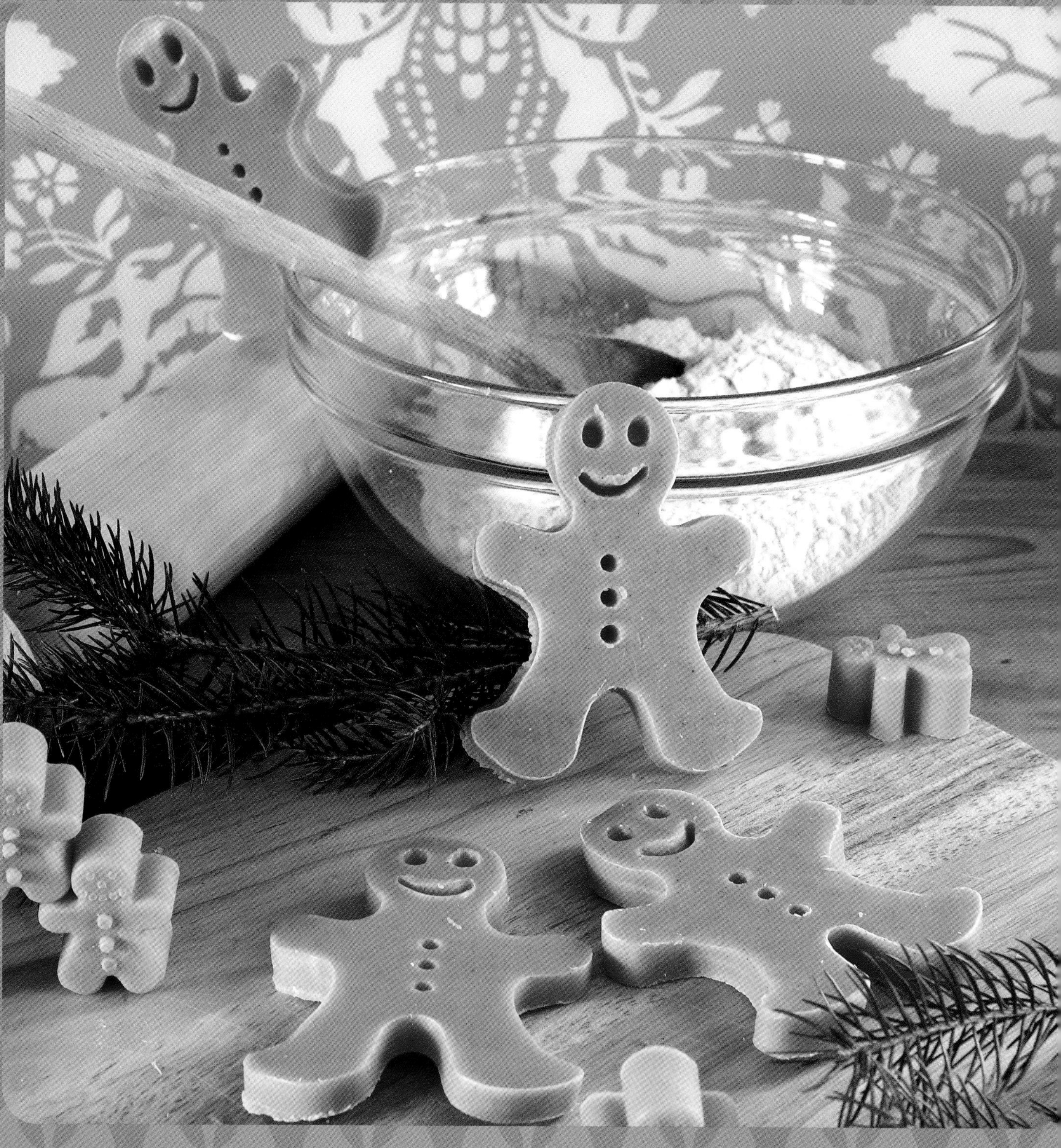

You're sure of a warm welcome from the Gingerbread family, with their spicy and comforting aroma. These make great gifts and are fun for children – just make sure they know they can't eat them.

Mr & Mrs Gingerbread

See pages 24–35 for basic soap recipe instructions

Ingredients
900ml or 900g (32oz) melted white soap base
¼ to ½ a teaspoon liquid orange colour
½ teaspoon ginger powder
½ teaspoon cinnamon powder
3 teaspoons ginger oil, or a spicy fragrance oil

Moulds
Mini ice cube or cookie mould
Alternative: baking tray with cookie cutters

CAUTION: Make sure these soaps are clearly labelled 'do not eat' and keep them away from children and animals.

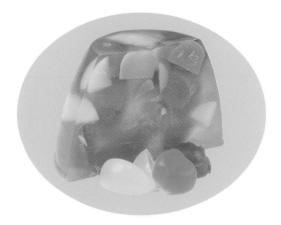

Are you feeling fruity? This mouth-wateringly juicy recipe is a favourite of children and adults alike, and everyone will want to take a slice home.

Fruit Salad

See pages 24–35 for basic soap recipe instructions

Ingredients
For the fruit embeds
Small quantity of clear soap base
Red, yellow and green liquid colour

For the fruit bowl
1 litre or 1kg (35oz) melted clear soap base.
4 teaspoons Tropicana (or other clear fruity fragrance oil)

Moulds
Fruit-shaped ice cube moulds for embeds
Plastic pudding basin or glass pudding basin lined
    with food wrap

Instructions
Colour small batches of clear soap base appropriately for each fruit (green for apple, red for strawberry, yellow for lemons etc). Make the small fruit embeds and allow to set.

For the fruit bowl, make the clear soap base. Spritz the fruit-shaped soap embeds, pour a little of the clear soap into the bottom of the mould and add some fruit soaps. Repeat until the mould is full.

If you do not have fruit-shaped ice cube moulds, use a plain ice cube tray to make rectangular coloured chunks. Plastic basins from ready-made steamed puddings are ideal for the fruit bowl.

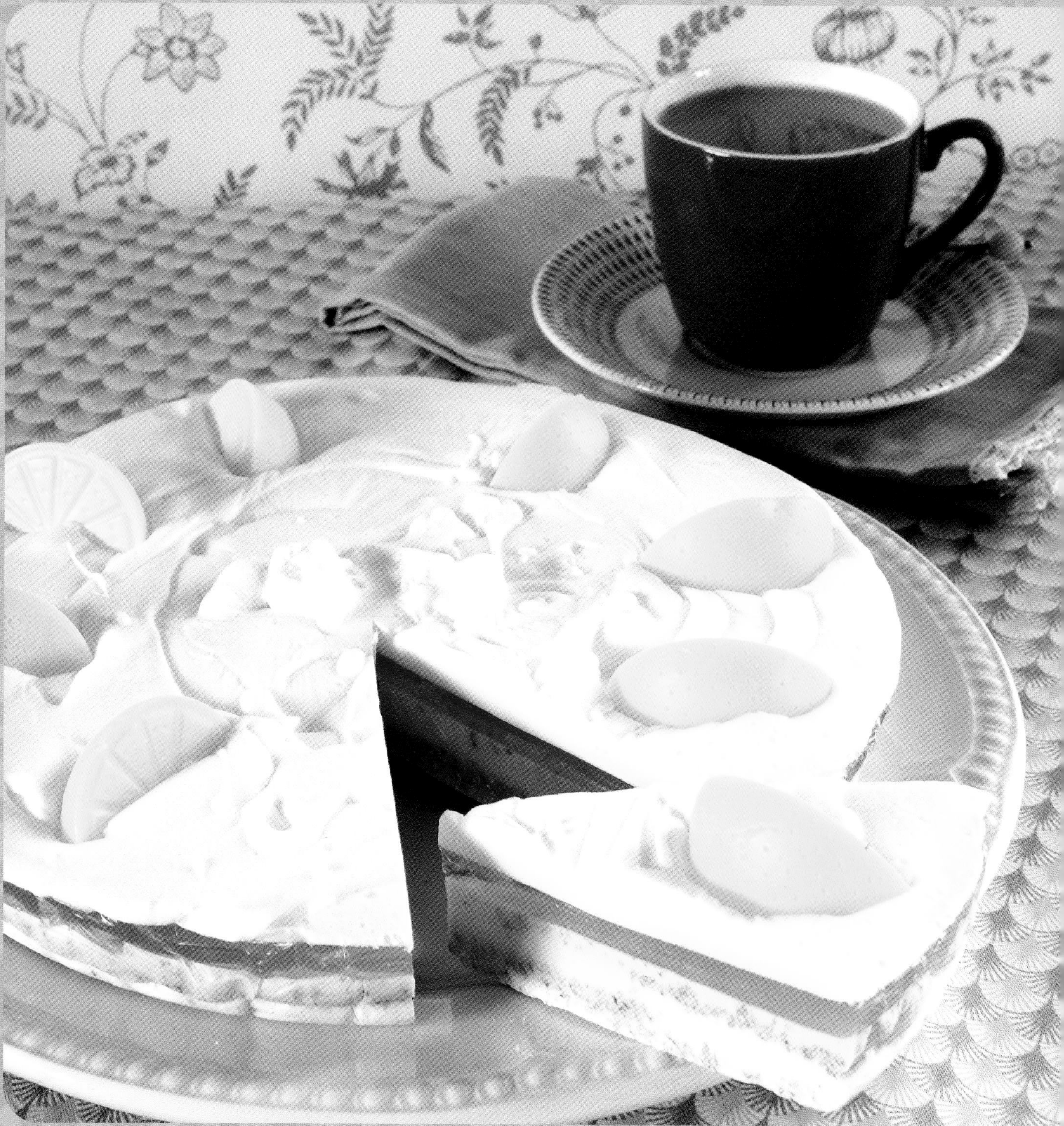

This one will really test your layering skills! The basic techniques in this recipe can be used to make all sorts of different pies, tarts or cakes, perfect for those who are watching their weight.

Easy as Pie

See pages 24–35 for basic soap recipe instructions

Ingredients

For the fruit embeds
Small quantity of white or clear soap base
Yellow liquid colouring

For the bottom layer
200ml or 200g (7oz) melted white soap base
6 tablespoons oats
1 teaspoon lemon essential oil or lemon meringue pie fragrance oil

For the middle layer
200ml or 200g (7oz) melted clear soap base
1 teaspoon lemon essential oil or lemon meringue pie fragrance oil
½ teaspoon yellow liquid colour

For the top layer
200ml or 200g (7oz) white soap base
½ teaspoon lemon essential oil or lemon meringue pie fragrance oil

Moulds
Lemon slice-shaped ice cube mould for the embeds.
Flan dish or tin lined with plastic food wrap.

Instructions
Using the lemon-slice shaped mould, make the fruit embeds – colour soap yellow and leave to set.
Bottom: pour into mould, leave until set slightly, but still warm.
Middle: spritz bottom layer and pour on the yellow middle layer.
Top: whip the soap to create texture, spritz and pour. Quickly spritz lemon slices and push into the top layer.

This soap is fun to keep by the kitchen sink to use after an afternoon of hard digging in the garden – no expensive moulds are used here but the end results are fantastic.

Totally Potty

See pages 24–35 for basic soap recipe instructions

Ingredients

500ml or 500g (17½oz) melted white soap base
1 teaspoon organic English lavender essential oil
½ teaspoon manuka essential oil
½ teaspoon bog myrtle essential oil
½ teaspoon avocado oil
½ teaspoon wheatgrass powder

Moulds

Plastic plant pot with the bottom securely taped up

Passed an exam? Reached a goal? Present this special soap scroll to a high achiever, or simply an all round-winner who deserves recognition. Make different-coloured layers and roll together for dramatic effect.

Award Winner

See pages 24–35 for basic soap recipe instructions

Ingredients

500ml or 500g (17½oz) melted white soap base
2 teaspoons rooibos (red bush) tea
¼ teaspoon myrrh essential oil
¼ teaspoon frankincense essential oil
¼ teaspoon vetiver essential oil
1 teaspoon neroli light
1 teaspoon argan oil
1 teaspoon annatto powder
   (or ½ teaspoon liquid yellow colour)

Additional instructions

Pour the soap into a lined tray and leave to set until only just set and still pliable. Take out the sheet of soap and cut in half. Taper each rectangle (see page 32 for instructions) and quickly roll up into a scroll.

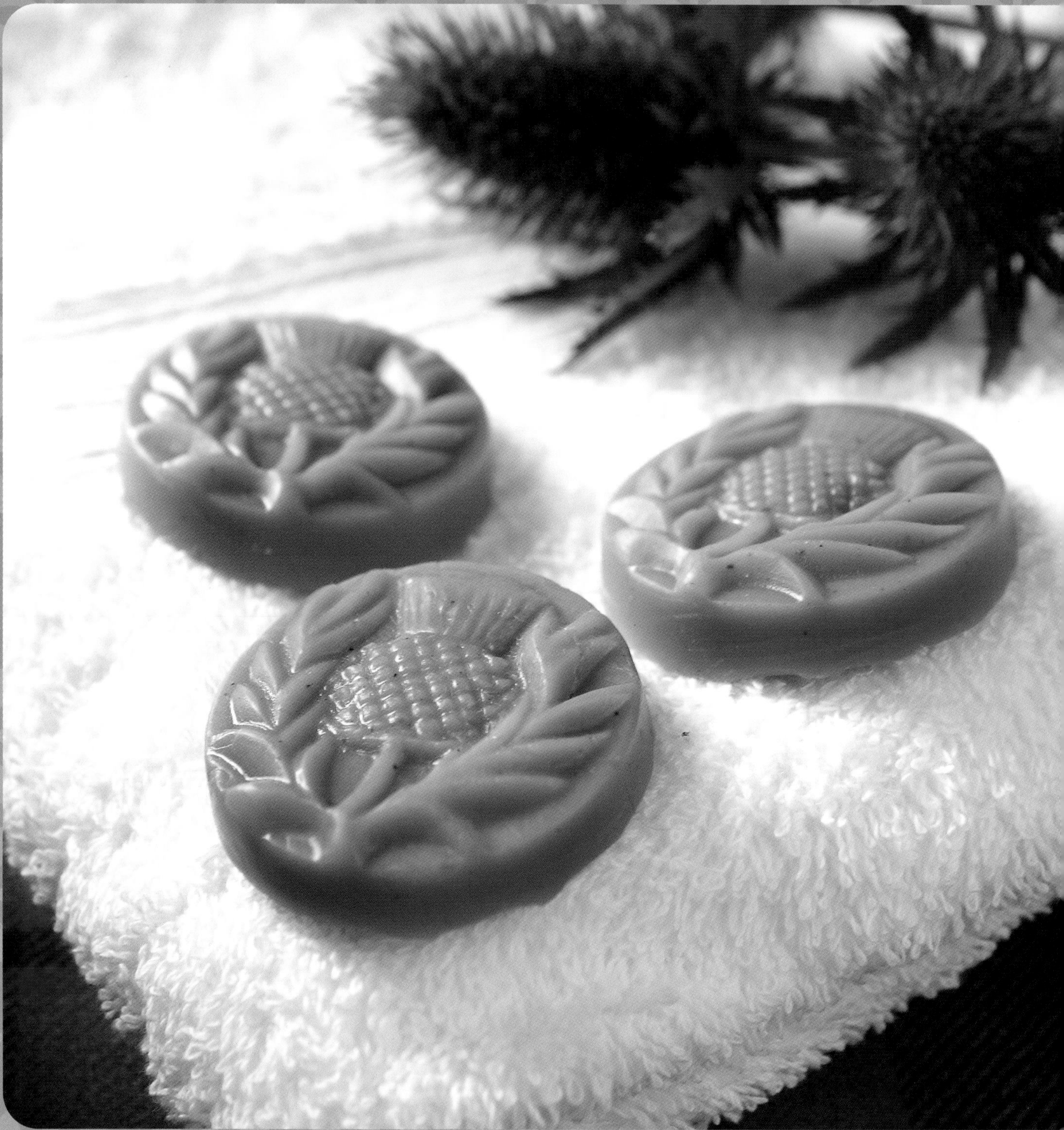

These cute little soaps made in guest-sized thistle moulds use the legendary properties of milk thistle, a herb that is beneficial to the liver, soothing to the skin and anti-inflammatory.

Thistle Do

See pages 24–35 for basic soap recipe instructions

Ingredients

200ml or 200g (7oz) melted white soap base
1 teaspoon Hawthorn and Heather fragrance oil
¼ teaspoon milk thistle powder
¼ teaspoon purple liquid colour (or alkanet powder)
½ teaspoon wheatgerm oil

Moulds

Guest-sized soap moulds with thistle detail

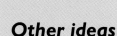

Other ideas
Use a small pastry cutter to cut out mini rounds of soap

The writing doesn't have to be on the wall: focus your artistic urges on this wacky recipe that uses leftover pieces of soap. Go mad and throw clashing colours together to create a masterpiece.

Graffiti

See pages 24–35 for basic soap recipe instructions

Ingredients

1 litre or 1kg (35oz) melted white soap base
Multi-coloured soap scraps left over from
    previous projects
2–3 teaspoons fragrance or essential oil of your choice
    such as Cool Breeze

Moulds

Any suitable plastic mould

Additional instructions

Pour some of the scented white base into the bottom of the mould. Chop up all the soap scraps and spritz with surgical spirit. Sprinkle the multi-coloured pieces into the white mixture. Pour in some more soap mixture, then add more scraps. Repeat until the mould is full for a fabulous multi-coloured confetti or graffiti effect.

Suppliers

Many pharmacies and health food shops supply essential oils and herbs for use in cosmetics, but you will need to purchase soap base from a soap ingredients supplier.

The following is a list of mail order/internet-based companies: the addresses provided are trading addresses, which are warehouses, and are not open to the public unless specified.

UK

Amphora Aromatics
www.amphora-aromatics.com
36 Cotham Hill
Cotham
Bristol
BS6 6LA
United Kingdom
Tel: + 44 (0) 117 904 7212
Fax + 44 (0) 117 940 5779
Wide range of essential oils and aromatherapy supplies

Aromantic Ltd
www.aromantic.co.uk
17 Tyler Street
Forres
Moray
IV36 1EL
United Kingdom
Tel: +44 (0) 1309 696900
Fax: +44 (0) 1309 696911
All soap-making ingredients and moulds

Bach™ Original Flower Remedies
www.bachremedies.co.uk
Head Office, Nelsons House
83 Parkside
Wimbledon
London
SW19 5LP
United Kingdom
Tel: +44 (0) 20 8780 4200
Fax: +44 (0) 20 8789 0141
Bach Flower Remedies are also available from many pharmacies and health food shops

Bathbomb.biz Limited
www.bathbomb.biz
Unit 4, Bessemer Road
Basingstoke
Hampshire
RG21 3NB
United Kingdom
Tel: +44 (0) 1256 474889
All soap-making ingredients and moulds

Cakes Cookies & Crafts Shop
www.cakescookiesandcraftsshop.co.uk
Unit 2, Francis Business Park
White Lund Industrial Estate
Morecambe
Lancashire
LA3 3PT
United Kingdom
Tel: +44 (0) 1524 389684
Huge range of fun chocolate moulds

G. Baldwin & Co
www.baldwins.co.uk
171/173 Walworth Road
London
SE17 1RW
United Kingdom
Tel: +44 (0)20 7703 5550
Fax: +44 (0)20 7252 6264
Herb specialists established in 1844: vast range of herbs and a high street shop

Gracefruit
www.gracefruit.com
146 Glasgow Road
Longcroft
Stirlingshire
FK4 1QL
United Kingdom
Tel: +44 (0) 1324 841353
Skype: gracefruit.com
A wide range of soap-making ingredients, soap bases and essential oils plus unusual and interesting ingredients and fragrances

Just A Soap
www.justasoap.co.uk
Century Unit 7, Brunel Way
Thetford
Norfolk
IP24 1HP
United Kingdom
Tel: +44 (0) 1284 735043
All soap-making Ingredients and moulds

Sheabutter Cottage
www.sheabuttercottage.co.uk
Unit 3, Sonning Farm
Charvil Lane
Sonning
Reading
RG4 6RH
United Kingdom
Tel: + 44 (0) 20 8144 4609
Fairtrade oils, butters, essential oils and other ingredients

Soap Basics
www.soapbasics.co.uk
23 Southbrook Road
Melksham
Wiltshire
SN12 8DS
United Kingdom
Tel: + 44 (0) 1225 899286
E-mail: info@soapbasics.co.uk
A wide range of ingredients, fragrances, additives, colour, lots of unusual moulds and wide selection of micas

The Soap Kitchen
www.thesoapkitchen.co.uk
Units 2 D&E Hatchmoor Industrial Estate
Hatchmoor Road
Torrington
Devon
EX38 7HP
United Kingdom
Tel: +44 (0) 1805 622944.
Fax: +44 (0) 870 4586724.
Email: info@thesoapkitchen.co.uk
A wide range of ingredients, soap bases, moulds, oils, butters, colour, herbs. Large range of fragrances

The Soapmakers Store
www.soapmakers-store.com
Unit 3, Quatro Park
Blakelands Industrial Estate
Tanners Drive
Milton Keynes
MK14 5FJ
United Kingdom
Tel: + 44 (0) 1908 334108
Fax: + 44 (0) 1908 566988
All soap-making ingredients and moulds

Soap School
www.soapschool.com
20 The Grove
Fartown
Huddersfield
West Yorkshire
HD2 1BL
United Kingdom
Tel +44 (0)1484 310014
Email: sarah.janes3@ntlworld.com
Large supply of moulds including a bespoke service

US and Canada

Bramble Berry Inc.
www.brambleberry.com
2138 Humboldt Street
Bellingham
WA 98225 USA
Tel: 360-734-8278 Toll Free: 877-627-7883
Fax: 360-752-0992
Huge range of soap-making ingredients, fragrances, oils and moulds

Camden-Grey Essential Oils Inc.
www.camdengrey.com
3579 NW 82 Ave.
Doral, FL 33122 USA
Toll Free Line for orders only: 866-503-8615
Tel: 305-500-9630
Fax: 305-500-9425
Email: customerservice@camdengrey.com
Wide range of essential oils, absolutes and moulds

The Chemistry Store
www.chemistrystore.com
The Chemistry Store
1133 Walter Price St
Cayce, SC 29033
Toll Free: 800-224-1430
Fax: 803-926-5389
Email: Sales – sales@chemistrystore.com
Order enquires – glitter@chemistrystore.com
All soap-making ingredients

Cranberry Lane
www.cranberrylane.com
150 - 2268 No 5 Rd.
Richmond, BC
V6X 2T1 Canada
Toll Free: 1-800-833-4533
Local: 604-944-1488
Large supply of ingredients and moulds

Custom Chocolate Shop
www.customchocolateshop.com
RR 2 Box 2378
Canadensis, PA 18325 USA
Email: kristin@customchocolateshop.com
Large range of chocolate moulds including personalised moulds

The Essential Oil Company
www.essentialoil.com
8225 SE 7th Ave
Portland
Oregon 97202 USA
Toll Free: 800-729-5912
Tel Local: 503-872-8735 – Outside US 503-872-8772
Fax: 503-872-8767
Essential oils and moulds

From Nature With Love
www.fromnaturewithlove.com
Natural Sourcing, LLC
341 Christian Street, Oxford, CT 06478 USA
Tel: 800-520-2060 or 203-702-2500
Fax: 203-702-2501
Soap bases, all ingredients, moulds and pre-made mini soap embeds

Kangaroo Blue
www.kangarooblue.com
PO Box 9021
Naperville, IL 60567-9021 USA
Tel: 630-999-8132
Fax: 847-589-1079
Soap bases, all ingredients, starter kits and equipment kits
Email: info@kangarooblue.com

Majestic Mountain Sage
www.thesage.com (look under Catalog)
2490 South 1350
West Nibley, Utah 84321 USA
Tel: 435-755-0863
Fax: 435-755-2108
Soap bases and all other soap-making ingredients and moulds

Milky Way Molds
www.milkywaymolds.com
Box 507
4207 SE Woodstock
Portland, OR 97206 USA
Tel: 800-588-7930
Fax: 202-330-4563
Email: contact@milkywaymolds.com
Designers and manufacturers of a huge range of unique, fun moulds

The Scent Works
www.scent-works.com
PO Box 828
Durham
North Carolina
27702-0828 USA
Tel: 1-973-598-9600
Fax: 1-973-532-0858
Email: Sales@TheScentworks.com
Large range of fragrance and essential oils, herbs, oils, butters and botanicals

Australia and New Zealand

Aussie Soap Supplies
www.aussiesoapsupplies.com.au
PO Box 165
Palmyra WA 6957
Visits to workshop by appointment
Tel: +61 (0)8 9339 1885
Fax: +61 (0)8 9339 7947
Soap base, moulds and other soap-making ingredients

Big Tree Supplies
www.bigtreesupplies.com.au
89 Emerald Street
Murarrie QLD 4172
Tel +61 (0)7 3907 0938
Email: info@bigtreesupplies.com.au
Moulds

Heirloom Body Care
www.heirloombodycare.com.au
78 Barnes Road
Llandilo NSW 2747
Visitors by appointment
Tel: +61 (0)2 4777 4457
Fax: +61 (0)2 4777 4873
Email: heirloom@heirloombodycare.com.au
Soap bases and many other supplies for soap making

Nature Shop
www.natureshop.com.au
10 Japonica Road,
Epping, NSW 2121
Tel: +61 (0)2 98691807
Fax: +61 (0)2 98692669
E-mail: info@natureshop.com.au
Essential oils, botanicals and oils

Australian Bush Flower Essences

Snowdrift Farm, Inc.
www.snowdriftfarm.com
4420 N. Highway Drive
Tucson, AZ 85705 USA
Tel: 1-520-887-9431
Fax: 520-292-5039
Wide range of all soap-making essentials

www.ausflowers.com.au
Bush Biotherapies Pty Ltd
45 Booralie Road,
Terrey Hills, NSW 2084
Tel: +61 (0)2 9450 1388
Fax: +61 (0)2 9450 2866
E-Mail: info@ausflowers.com.au

Essential Oils and Soap
www.oilsandsoap.com.au
PO Box 191
Beaconsfield
Tas 7270
Tel: +61 (0)3 6383 1284
Email: info@oilsandsoap.com.au
Soap base, moulds and other soap-making ingredients

Manuka Oil.com
www.manukaoil.com
Bio-Extracts Limited.
PO Box 5,
187 Mill Road,
Bombay, South Auckland,
New Zealand.
Tel: +64 9 236 0917
Fax: +64 9 236 0918
Email: email@ManukaOil.com
Manuka oil

About the author

Elaine Stavert formed The Littlecote Soap Co after a life-changing move from her television career in London to a farm in the beautiful Buckinghamshire countryside. Surrounded by hedgerows and meadows, and with a keen interest in herbalism and aromatherapy, Elaine was soon developing a range of natural toiletries and bath products that were both kind to the skin and quintessentially English. Elaine's passion for her products is evident in the pure and natural ingredients that are used in imaginative ways to produce traditional recipes with contemporary twists.

The Littlecote Soap Co.
Littlecote Farm
Littlecote
Nr Dunton
Buckingham
MK18 3LN
www.littlecotesoap.co.uk

Acknowledgements

Robert, my mother and Pearl
For love, encouragement and support.

I would also like to thank my wonderful team at The Littlecote Soap Co., Caroline Heron, Nikki Jellis, Rebecca Gulliver, Carole Capel , Andrea Ellis and Jess Bliss for their hard work and dedication and for the use of their hands in the book. My thanks also to all those at Littlecote Farm: Alison Vinter in the office, Sean Jackman and Mr Nab for their sense of humour and for introducing me to a whole new array of natural aromas. Sue Lister from Lister Communications, Sarah Janes from Soap School, Richard Phillips from The Soap Kitchen, Lisa Wright from The Gallery and Michael Bevens for their shining pearls of wisdom and professional advice. And finally to Benjamin Hedges from J. Hedges and Sons for reminding us of traditional values and without whom the company would not exist.

My grateful thanks also to the talented team at GMC Publications, for Jonathan Bailey and Gerrie Purcell for inviting me to write this book, to Gilda Pacitti and Jo Patterson for their creative eye for detail and design, Hedda Roennevig for picture research and much more, and editors Virginia Brehaut and Alison Howard for their skill, professionalism and patience.

Photographic acknowledgements

Main project photography by Laurel Guilfoyle

Step-by-step photography by Elaine Stavert and also on pages: 11, 18, 23, 24, 34 (right), 36, 39 (right), 40, 41 (right), 43 (right), 45, 47, 49 (left), 50, 67, 73 (bottom two left column, right column), 79, 81 (left), 83, 84 (centre and right).

All other photography by Anthony Bailey, except as below:

GMC Publications would like to thank the following for pictures used in this book:
Allie Caulfield/Flickr: page 13 (right) and page 15 (right);
Flickr: page 80 (right), 82 (left) and 85; Japan Ryokan Association: page 13 (left);
Jonrawlinson/Flickr: page 58; London Midland and Scottish Railway Company/
The Commons: page 15 (left); Michael Bevens: page 40 (left);
www.morguefile.com: page 73 (left column, top two);
Stahrdust3/Flickr: page 14 (bottom right);
www.toast.co.uk: page 12 (top left) and page 14 (top left);
U.S. Library of Congress/The Commons: page 16; Vanessa Yvonne/Flickr: page 18
Virginia Brehaut, page 62

GMC Publications would also like to thank the following people who
kindly loaned props for photography:
Steamer Trading Ltd, Lewes, East Sussex
Andrea Hargreaves, Virginia Brehaut, Gill Parris, Emma Bennett,
Lucy Emmett, Hedda Roennevig, Elaine Stavert,
Laurel Guilfoyle, and Wickle, Lewes, East Sussex.

Index

Names of recipes are given in italics.

Contact us for a complete catalogue, or visit our website:

GMC Publications Ltd, 166 High Street, Lewes, East Sussex BN7 1XU, United Kingdom

Tel: +44 (0)1273 488005 Fax: +44 (0)1273 402866

www.gmcbooks.com